THE RELEVANCE OF

INTERNATIONAL

ADJUDICATION

THE RELEVANCE OF

INTERNATIONAL

ADJUDICATION

by Milton Katz

HARVARD UNIVERSITY PRESS

CAMBRIDGE, MASSACHUSETTS

1968

PREFATORY NOTE

The Relevance of International Adjudication is based on a series of six lectures by the author given in a special Program of Instruction for Lawyers conducted by the Harvard Law School in Honolulu, Hawaii, July 17 to 29, 1967, under the co-sponsorship of the University of Hawaii and the Bar Association of Hawaii.

CONTENTS

THE RELEVANCE OF

INTERNATIONAL

ADJUDICATION

CHAPTER ONE

SCOPE AND PURPOSE

In the *Great God Brown,* Eugene O'Neill spoke his torment through the lips of Billy Brown: "Man is born broken. He lives by mending. The grace of God is glue." At levels closer to the surface of human experience than the depths O'Neill sought to probe, man has tried to use the law as glue, not without some measure of success. Man has mended with law and attempted to mend in diverse ways that correspond to the many functions of law. Here, I touch only two of the functions. They are elemental: to curb violence and to resolve controversies.

There are limits to effective action through law that are fundamental, embedded in its nature. The limits govern the possible use of law to settle disputes. Lawyers are familiar with the question of what makes a controversy justiciable. The question arises at more than one level. In practical professional terms, it is a question of whether a controversy comes within the particular competence of a particular court to adjudicate, as defined by a particular statutory or constitutional provision. In more general and basic terms, it is a question of what there is in the nature of a controversy that makes it amenable, or not amenable, to adjudication by any court. In the latter sense, the question turns on what is meant by adjudication. The analysis is governed by conscious or unconscious premises concerning the meaning and reach of law.

Lawyers normally pursue their calling well within the ultimate limits of law. Within the limits, the law has its defects in practice and its overlay of cant. Perry Miller, in his posthumous study, *The Life of the Mind in America,* has reminded us of the exasperation provoked in early Americans by the shibboleths of the law and the flaws in its application.[1] A popular irritation with law and lawyers sounded in American prose and verse from the American Revolution to the Civil War. Many Americans today would relish the sting of Carl Sandburg's "tell me why a hearse horse snickers hauling a lawyer's bones."[2] The literature and folk adages of other peoples give evidence that the sentiment is widely shared. Yet, for all the shortcomings, the legal systems of civilized states represent mankind's longest and most highly tested endeavor to restrain violence and settle human conflict through orderly processes on the basis of principle.

In an address before the National Press Club on February 18, 1960, the late Secretary of State Christian A. Herter projected a "second stage of general disarmament." He proposed that the objective in this second stage be: "First, to create certain universally accepted rules of law which, if followed, would prevent all nations from attacking other nations." His proposal exemplified an ancient and tenacious human hope, to apply the experience of domestic law to the no man's land between states.

Within a society, law gives effect to patterns of belief and

---

[1] Perry Miller, *The Life of the Mind in America* (New York: Harcourt, Brace & World, Inc., 1965), pp. 99-104.

[2] Carl Sandburg, "The Lawyers Know Too Much," in *Selected Poems of Carl Sandburg,* ed. Rebecca West (New York: Harcourt, Brace and Co., 1926), p. 200.

purpose through rules of conduct and an apparatus of administration. In the use of law to resolve disputes and prevent or contain violence, administration centers in the courts and the police. Men anxious to restrain international aggression and end international disputes peaceably have long sought to invoke international rules, policing and adjudication. They have also tried to regularize the forms and procedures of international political relationships. Twice within the past half century, they have undertaken to build world organizations to keep the peace, or at least reduce the incidence and the scale of war.

As the lives of legal systems and organized societies are measured, international law is young. Although it contains elements from sources in Roman law, Greek philosophy, and medieval Christian doctrine, its beginnings are usually traced to the period between the middle of the sixteenth and the middle of the seventeenth centuries, marked by the writings of Francisco de Vitoria, Francisco Suarez, and Grotius, and by the Treaty of Westphalia. It emerged in Europe along with the modern nation-state and modern notions of state sovereignty. Developing slowly, it remained essentially a product of the diplomatic practice and political and legal thought of Europe until the nineteenth century, when it received a gathering increment from the United States and Latin America. Yet it was conceived, and its mission projected, in universal terms.

To be vindicated as a universal system in the twentieth century, international law had to take account of the thought and practice of the new or transformed states of Asia and Africa, as well as of the Communist nations which trumpeted their rejection of some of the ultimate premises of Western government and law. It also had to survive two world wars, and cope with an overwhelming technology and constant change engendered by the continuing scientific and industrial revolutions. Such an accommodation would have strained the capacity of even the most mature and highly tested legal system, supporting and sustained by the most resourceful diplomacy. Unfortunately, international law, despite the promise of its growth, entered the twentieth century still comparatively rudimentary in its doctrine and institutions. Established diplomacy, if more serviceable than international law, itself required new development in its structure and method. A mutation was needed to give a new direction to the evolution of international law and diplomacy.

A mutation occurred. Designated "international organization," it represents a variation of an instrument long familiar to international law and diplomacy—a treaty. An "international organization"—more precisely an international governmental organization—originates in a multilateral treaty among a group of nations. It may be worldwide or regional. Typically, the participating states accept obligations for a period of indefinite duration; take part through delegations constituted on a uniform basis, with some continuity of form and function; meet at regular intervals in organs of deliberation, according to a prescribed procedure; and establish a common administration, manned by personnel whose duties are defined by the purposes of the treaty and are owed to the group of member states as a whole. The common administration is usually called a secretariat. The term "organization" is sometimes applied to the member states as a group. More accurately, it describes the composite of delegations, deliberative organs, and secretariat. It is sometimes loosely applied to the secretariat.

There are specimens of the mutation that antedate the twentieth century. The oldest that still exist are the Central Commission for the Navigation of the Rhine, which originated at the Congress of Vienna in 1815, and the Danube Commission, created in its earliest form at the Congress of Paris in 1856. The Universal Postal Union dates from 1874, the International Union of Weights and Measures from 1875, the World Meteorological Organization from 1878, the International Union for the Protection of Personal Property from 1883, and the International Union for the Protection of Literary and Artistic Works from 1886. The earliest precursor of the Organization of American States came into being in 1890 when, at the First International Conference of American States, eighteen nations of North and South America formed the International Union of American Republics "for the prompt collection and distribution of commercial information."[3] It operated through its "Commercial Bureau," renamed the Pan American Union in 1910.

At the beginning of the 1960's, over one hundred and twenty international organizations existed.[4] Of these, three fifths had been created since 1940; and a number of those that antedated World War II had since undergone constitu-

---

[3] Carnegie Endowment for International Peace, *The International Conferences of American States, 1889-1928,* ed. J. B. Scott (New York: Oxford University Press, 1931), p. 36.

[4] Amos J. Peaslee and Dorothy Peaslee Xydis, *International Governmental Organizations—Constitutional Documents,* 2d ed. (The Hague: Martinus Nijhoff, 1961), I, xxxii. The authors counted 122.

tional revision. "More than four fifths of the basic constitutional documents [for international organizations] . . . in force [in 1961] (103 out of a total of 122)" were barely twenty years old, dating from no later than the beginning of World War II.[5] Their functions are legion, ranging from "agriculture, animals and their diseases, arbitration, banking, coal and steel, cotton, customs" through "liquor traffic, literary and artistic works, marine life, meteorological observations, migrants, money, navigation, patents" to "trade names, uniform laws, weights and measures, whaling and wheat."[6]

All have contributed in some way and in some degree to the evolution of international law. It remains to see how significant the mutation may have made international law for its central concern, the peaceful and constructive settlement of international disputes. I shall try to probe a few points within the international experience after World War II that may yield a clue. My focus will be upon international adjudication and related processes. I shall concentrate upon disputes within the experience of the United Nations, as the principal international organization; within the record of the International Court, as the principal international judicial tribunal; and within the range of tensions between the free and the Communist states, and between established industrial states and newly emerging states or peoples that "have not yet attained a full measure of self-government,"[7] as two of the dominant themes in international affairs since the end of World War II.

5 *Ibid.*
6 *Ibid.*, pp. xxxviii-xxxix.
7 See United Nations Charter, Art. 73.

CHAPTER TWO

THE COLD WAR AND THE

PEACEFUL SETTLEMENT

OF DISPUTES

In the two decades since the end of World War II, American conduct, whether within or outside the United Nations or the Organization of American States, alone or in alliance with others, has revealed a consistent pattern of behavior in regard to Soviet Russian or Communist Chinese expansionism. The United States has resisted attempts by the Soviet Union or Communist China to extend their dominion or sphere of control by force or threats of force or by the support of force or threats on the part of others. If and when peacekeeping measures or measures of pacific settlement coincided with a policy of resistance, the United States used them happily. If peacekeeping and pacific settlement did not coincide with resistance, the policy of resistance prevailed. To American eyes, this policy was fundamentally consistent with the cause of peace with justice and freedom. In the view of the United States, peace with justice and freedom could not be safeguarded against Soviet Russian or Communist Chinese expansionism by peacekeeping measures or measures of peaceful settlement except within the frame of reference established by unrelenting resistance. The United

States was ready to carry resistance to the point of the actual
use of force, as in Korea and Vietnam; to the point of an explicit show of readiness to use force, as in the Cuban missile
crisis; or to the point of support for the armed force of
others, as in Greece.

International law played its part in fixing the frame of
reference for each dispute. Treaties and customary international law defined the geographical reach of Cuba and its
territorial waters, the boundaries of Guatemala crossed by
the invading insurgents in 1954, and the geographical spheres
of North and South Korea. If they did not define, they nevertheless pervaded the notions of blockade that affected the
attitudes of other states toward the quarantine declared by
the United States around Cuba in 1962, as well as the notions
of supervening air and outer space from which were derived
the political and psychological implications of the flights by
the U2 over the fields and cities of the Soviet Union.

The adversaries could and sometimes did use international
law in asserting their claims. Cuba could cite international
law in support of its right as a state to enter into relations
with another state of its own choosing (the Soviet Union);
in support of its right to acquire goods or services from another state; and in support of its right to place goods so acquired on its own territory. The United States could contend
that, under Article 6 of the Inter-American Treaty of Reciprocal Assistance,[1] signed by Cuba, the Organ of Consultation
must meet immediately in order to agree on the measures
which must be taken whenever "the inviolability or the integrity of the territory or the sovereignty or political inde-

1 TIAS 1838 (Dec. 3, 1948), 21 UNTS 93 (1948).

pendence of any American State should be affected by an aggression which is not an armed attack or by an extra-continental or intra-continental conflict, or by any other fact or situation that might endanger the peace of America." The United States also could and in due course did point to Article 8 of the same treaty which authorized the Organ of Consultation to adopt as remedial measures any "one or more of the following: recall of chiefs of diplomatic missions; breaking of diplomatic relations; breaking of consular relations; partial or complete interruption of economic relations or of rail, sea, air, postal, telegraphic, telephonic, and radiotelephonic or radiotelegraphic communications; and use of armed force." Cuba would deny that the integrity of the territory or the political independence of any American state was endangered or that indeed there was any "fact or situation" for which it was responsible that might threaten the peace of America. On the contrary, it would insist that the missiles it installed were there to defend it against precisely such a threat from the United States of America.

The Soviet Union fulminated against a violation of its territory by the American U2, but sought to justify the invasion of South Korea by North Korea as well as the support of guerillas fomenting civil warfare in Greece by groups in Albania, Yugoslavia, and Bulgaria. The United States invoked the United Nations Charter against the violation of South Korean territory; but it acknowledged the U2 flight as its own, and it supported the invasion of Guatemala against the Arbenz regime from Honduras and Nicaragua.

Whatever the function of international law as part of the setting of a dispute, and whatever the attempts to muster international law in support of rival claims, the parties in Cold War disputes have not resorted to adjudication under international law as a means to settle their disputes. Their aversion is not confined to adjudication in the strict sense. It extends to arbitration and, beyond arbitration, to any efforts of impartial third parties to arrange an accommodation through flexible and orderly procedures guided by their skill and discretion.

The rejection of adjudication and arbitration in Cold War disputes represents the legal aspect of a pattern of behavior dominated by its political aspect. It remains to consider whether the legal aspect is anything more than a mechanical reflection of the political. It would be no more if the pattern of behavior merely expresses the willful unruliness of states that repudiate international law both as it is and as it might be. International law is a consensual legal system. It is consensual in a practical and operational sense, which is not to be confused with the abstract notion of consent assumed in the philosophical concept of the social contract. It derives from the consent of states expressed in treaties and a consensus among states implicit in a settled course of state practice. If states should want no part of it, that would end the matter. I believe, however, that the legal aspect may reveal something more. It will be useful to inquire how far the apparent irrelevance of international adjudication or arbitration to the settlement of Cold War disputes may result from the absence of tribunals to determine and apply the law; or, if tribunals exist, from their lack of adequate means to assert their authority; or, if the means exist, from the tribunal's lack of a will to use the means available. How far may the apparent irrelevance result from some inadequacy in the content of international law as the law then stands? How far may the irrelevance derive from limitations inherent in the nature of adjudication, as exhibited by older and more highly evolved legal systems than international law?

In a brief and preliminary way, I shall examine these questions and concentrate upon the last, which I believe will lead to the heart of the matter. I shall consider it first in relation to the legal system best known to us, which exists as part of a political entity far more tightly organized and powerful, and far more profoundly accepted by its people, than any international order or international organization. I have in mind, of course, American law and the United States of America. The examination will focus upon the behavior of the American government and the role of its legal system when the cold war over slavery between North and South became hot and bloody. It may help to look again at the issues as they appeared to the participants.

Here is a statement of a Southern view, by a Convention held at Milledgeville, Georgia, in 1850. The Convention desired "that the position of this State may be clearly apprehended by her Confederates of the South and of the North, and that she may be blameless of all future consequences." To this end, the Convention states the views that it attributes to the people of Georgia:

> *First.* That we hold the American Union secondary in importance only to the rights and principles it was designed to perpetuate. That past associations, present

fruition, and future prospects, will bind us to it so long as it continues to be the safe-guard of those rights and principles . . .

Fourth. That the State of Georgia, in the judgment of this Convention, will and ought to resist, even (as a last resort) to a disruption of every tie which binds her to the Union, any future Act of Congress abolishing Slavery in the District of Columbia, without the consent and petition of the slave-holders thereof, or any Act abolishing Slavery in places within the slave-holding States, purchased by the United States for the erection of forts, magazines, arsenals, dock-yards, navy-yards, and other like purposes; or in any Act suppressing the slave-trade between slave-holding States.[2]

Eight years later, in the "House Divided" speech, on June 16, 1858, Abraham Lincoln stated his view of the matter: "I believe this government cannot endure, permanently half slave and half free. I do not expect the Union to be dissolved; I do not expect the house to fall; but I do expect it will cease to be divided. It will become all one thing, or all the other. Either the opponents of slavery will arrest the further spread of it, and place it where the public mind shall rest in the belief that it is in the course of ultimate extinction; or its advocates will push it forward, till it shall become alike lawful in all the States, old as well as new, North as well as South."[3]

---

2 Georgia Platform of 1850, in Alexander H. Stephens, *A Constitutional View of the Late War between the States* (Philadelphia: National Publishing Co., 1870), II, 676-677.

3 *Abraham Lincoln: His Writings and Speeches,* ed. Roy P. Basler (Cleveland and New York: World Publishing Co., 1946), pp. 372-373.

The Republican Party platform of May 16, 1860, carried forward the definition of these issues:

2. That the maintenance of the principles promulgated in the Declaration of Independence and embodied in the Federal constitution—"that all men are created equal; that they are endowed by their Creator with certain unalienable rights; that among these are life, liberty and the pursuit of happiness . . ." is essential to the preservation of our republican institutions; and that the Federal constitution, the rights of the states, and the union of the states, must and shall be preserved . . .

7. That the dogma that the constitution of its own force, carried slavery into any or all of the territories of the United States, is a dangerous political heresy, . . . is revolutionary in its tendency, and subversive of the peace and harmony of the country.

8. That the normal condition of all the territory of the United States is that of freedom; . . . it becomes our duty, by legislation, whenever such legislation is necessary, to maintain this provision of the constitution against all attempts to violate it; and we deny the authority of Congress, of a territorial legislature, or of any individual, to give legal existence to slavery in any territory of the United States.[4]

By a resolution adopted on November 30, 1860, the legislature of Mississippi, reaffirming the contentions of the

---

[4] Emerson D. Fite, *The Presidential Campaign of 1860* (New York: The Macmillan Co., 1911), pp. 237-239.

Georgia Convention of 1850, cast them more precisely into the mold of law:

> *Whereas,* The Constitutional Union was formed by the several States in their separate sovereign capacity for the purpose of mutual advantage and protection;
>
> That the several States are distinct sovereignties, whose supremacy is limited so far only as the same has been delegated by voluntary compact to a Federal Government, and when it fails to accomplish the ends for which it was established, the parties to the compact have the right to resume, each State for itself, such delegated power . . .
>
> That they have elected a majority of Electors for President and Vice-President on the ground that there exists an irreconcilable conflict between the two sections of the Confederacy in reference to their respective systems of labor and in pursuance of their hostility to us and our institutions, thus declaring to the civilized world that the powers of this Government are to be used for the dishonor and overthrow of the Southern Section of this great Confederacy. Therefore,
>
> *Be is resolved by the Legislature of the State of Mississippi,* That in the opinion of those who now constitute the said Legislature, the secession of each aggrieved State is the proper remedy for these injuries.[5]

President Buchanan had his own view of the matter. The process of secession had already begun, but it all could be

---

5 Mississippi, Laws of the State, 1860 (Jackson, Mississippi, 1860) 43-45.

straightened out if people would live and let live: "How easy would it be for the American people to settle the slavery question forever and to restore peace and harmony to this distracted country! They, and they alone, can do it. All that is necessary to accomplish the object, and all for which the slave States have ever contended, is to be let alone and permitted to manage their domestic institutions in their own way. As sovereign States, they, and they alone, are responsible before God and the world for the slavery existing among them. For this the people of the North are not more responsible and have no more right to interfere than with similar institutions in Russia or in Brazil."[6]

Buchanan carried his view of self-determination, 1860 style, even into his assessment of the powers of the President and the Congress:

> The question fairly stated is, Has the Constitution delegated to Congress the power to coerce a State into submission which is attempting to withdraw or has actually withdrawn from the Confederacy? If answered in the affirmative, it must be on the principle that the power has been conferred upon Congress to declare and to make war against a State. After much serious reflection I have arrived at the conclusion that no such power has been delegated to Congress or to any other department of the Federal Government . . .
>
> But if we possessed this power, would it be wise to exercise it under existing circumstances? The object

---

6 President James Buchanan, Fourth Annual Message, Dec. 3, 1860, in *Messages and Papers of the Presidents,* ed. James D. Richardson (Washington: GPO, 1897) V, 626, 627.

would doubtless be to preserve the Union. War would not only present the most effectual means of destroying it, but would vanish all hope of its peaceable reconstruction. Besides, in the fraternal conflict a vast amount of blood and treasure would be expended, rendering future reconciliation between the States impossible. In the meantime, who can foretell what would be the sufferings and privations of the people during its existence?

The fact is that our Union rests upon public opinion, and can never be cemented by the blood of its citizens shed in civil war. If it can not live in the affections of the people, it must one day perish. Congress possesses many means of preserving it by conciliation, but the sword was not placed in their hand to preserve it by force.[7]

For the final step in the definition of the issues, there is Lincoln's Message to Congress in Special Session on July 4, 1861:

At the beginning of the present Presidential term, four months ago, the functions of the Federal Government were found to be generally suspended within the several States of South Carolina, Georgia, Alabama, Mississippi, Louisiana, and Florida, excepting only those of the Post-Office Department . . .

. . . the purpose to sever the Federal Union was openly avowed. In accordance with this purpose, an ordinance had been adopted in each of these States declaring the

7 *Ibid.*, pp. 635, 636.

States respectively to be separated from the National Union . . .

So viewing the issue, no choice was left but to call out the war power of the Government and so to resist force employed for its destruction by force for its preservation . . .

They invented an ingenious sophism, which, if conceded, was followed by perfectly logical steps through all the incidents, to the complete destruction of the Union. The sophism itself is that any State of the Union may *consistently* with the National Constitution, and therefore *lawfully* and *peacefully,* withdraw from the Union without the consent of the Union or of any other State . . .

What is now combated is the position that secession is *consistent* with the Constitution—is *lawful* and *peaceful.* It is not contended that there is any express law for it, and nothing should ever be implied as law which leads to unjust or absurd consequences . . .

The seceders insist that our Constitution admits of secession.[8]

The Resolution of the state of Mississippi, President Buchanan's message, and President Lincoln's message explicitly defined legal issues. Mississippi affirmed the constitutional right of each state to retract the powers that it had delegated to the national government. Enumerating the alleged wrongs suffered by Mississippi, the legislature in

---

8 Abraham Lincoln, Special Session Message, July 4, 1861, in Richardson, *Messages and Papers of the Presidents,* VI, 20, 23, 26, 28. (The italics are Lincoln's.)

lawyer-like terms proclaimed that the "proper remedy" for
the "injuries" received by each "aggrieved State" was secession. President Buchanan "fairly stated" the central question to be whether the Constitution had "delegated to Congress the power to coerce a state into submission which is
attempting to withdraw or which has actually withdrawn
from the Confederacy." President Lincoln isolated the issue
that in his view went to the heart of the matter as "the
position that secession is *consistent* with the Constitution—
is *lawful* and *peaceful.*" In Lincoln's view, "no choice was
left but to call out the war power of the government." In the
message of July 4, 1861, Lincoln did not refer to an alternative possibility at least theoretically available, to submit
the issue as a question of constitutional law to the Supreme
Court of the United States.

Four months earlier, in his first inaugural address,
March 4, 1861, Lincoln, after affirming "the proposition
that in legal contemplation the Union is perpetual" and
"that no State upon its own mere motion can lawfully get
out of the Union," had taken account of "the position assumed by some that constitutional questions are to be decided by the Supreme Court" and that "such decisions must
be binding in any case upon the parties to a suit as to the
object of that suit, while they are also entitled to very high
respect and consideration in all parallel cases by all other
departments of the Government."[9] But he had earlier declared his opinion of the Dred Scott decision and in so doing
had implied a view of the position in which the decision
appeared to place the Supreme Court. "Let any one who

9 Richardson, *Messages and Papers of the Presidents*, VI, 5, 7, 9.

doubts, carefully contemplate that now almost complete legal combination—piece of machinery so to speak—compounded of the Nebraska doctrine, and the Dred Scott decision. Let him consider, not only what work the machinery is adapted to do, and how well adapted; but also, let him study the history of its construction, and trace, if he can, or rather fail, if he can, to trace the evidences of design, and concert of action, among its chief bosses, from the beginning . . . We cannot absolutely know that all these exact adaptations are the result of preconcert. But when we see a lot of framed timbers, different portions of which we know have been gotten out at different times and places and by different workmen . . . and we see these timbers joined together, and see they exactly make the frame of a house or a mill, all the tenons and mortises exactly fitting, . . . we find it impossible not to believe that [the several workmen] all understood one another from the beginning . . ."[10]

When Lincoln in his first inaugural address returned to an examination of "the position assumed by some, that constitutional questions are to be decided by the Supreme Court," and acknowledged the binding character of the Court's decisions in any case on the parties to the suit, he added: "At the same time, the candid citizen must confess that if the policy of the Government upon vital questions affecting the whole people is to be irrevocably fixed by decisions of the Supreme Court, the instant they are made in ordinary litigation between parties and personal actions the people will have ceased to be their own rulers, having to

[10] "House Divided" Speech, June 16, 1858, in Basler, *Abraham Lincoln*, pp. 373, 377.

that extent practically resigned their Government into the hands of that eminent tribunal. Nor is there in this view any assault upon the court or the judges. It is a duty from which they may not shrink to decide cases properly brought before them, and it is no fault of theirs if others seek to turn their decisions to political purposes."[11]

Had Lincoln been disposed to invoke the judicial power to resolve the legal issue, would the necessary institutions, doctrine, and procedures have been available? The Constitution existed. The Supreme Court existed. Under the famous language of Article 3, Section 2, the judicial power extended "to all Cases, in Law and Equity, arising under this Constitution . . . to Controversies to which the United States shall be a party;—to Controversies between two or more states." The Supreme Court had original jurisdiction in all cases "in which a State shall be Party." What if the United States had instituted a proceeding in the Supreme Court against, say, Georgia or Mississippi, praying that the Court adjudge the purported secession to be in violation of the Constitution and therefore void and of no effect, and asking that an appropriate decree issue enjoining the purported secession and requiring the defendant state to continue to behave as a member of the Union?

With the Civil War dominant in the national memory of the period, the question appears unreal. It may indeed be unreal, but if so, it is important to understand why. At least in a formal sense, such a proceeding could have been brought. If instituted, it would, I believe, have come to nothing, for reasons that I'll try to explain. But two cases in

11 Richardson, *Messages and Papers of the Presidents*, VI, 5, 9-10.

the Supreme Court, decided in 1868 and 1892, reveal that the explanation does not lie plainly visible on the surface of the judicial process. Both cases grew out of a protracted dispute between the United States and Texas. On May 2, 1890, Congress enacted a statute that provided in part as follows:

> That inasmuch as there is a controversy between the United States and the State of Texas as to the ownership of what is known as Greer Country . . . the Attorney General of the United States is hereby authorized and directed to commence in the name and on behalf of the United States, and prosecute to a final determination, a proper suit in equity in the Supreme Court of the United States against the State of Texas, setting forth the title and claim of the United States to the tract of land lying between the North and South Forks of the Red River where the Indian Territory and the State of Texas adjoin, . . . claimed by the State of Texas as within its boundary and part of its land, and designated on its map as Greer County . . . and said case shall be advanced on the docket of said court, and proceeded with to its conclusion as rapidly as the nature and circumstances of the case permit.[12]

The statute and the lawsuit were intended to bring to rest a dispute originating in a treaty between the United States and Spain made on February 22, 1819. The treaty defined the boundary line between the United States of

---

[12] 26 Stat. 81, 92, as cited in United States v. Texas, 143 U.S. 621-2, 12 S.Ct. 488 (1892).

America and Spanish territory in North America. In one provision, the treaty described the boundary line by reference to the course of the Red River and more particularly to a point where the thirty-second degree of latitude struck the Red River.

When Mexico became independent in 1824, negotiations for a new treaty were undertaken, and, in 1828, the boundaries defined by the treaty of 1819 were confirmed by an agreement between the United States and Mexico. When the Republic of Texas broke away from Mexico, a third treaty, between the United States and the Republic of Texas, was concluded on April 25, 1838, again confirming the boundaries originally defined in 1819. To prevent future disputes, the treaty of 1838 stipulated that each of the contracting parties—the Republic of Texas and the United States—would appoint commissioners and surveyors to mark out the lines on a map.

By an Act of Congress of September 9, 1850, disagreements that had arisen concerning the boundary were resolved in part by the renunciation of Texas to its claim to certain lands in exchange for the payment of $10,000,000 by the United States. But commissioners and surveyors in behalf of the parties were unable to resolve a dispute as to the meaning of the "Red River." The draftsmen of the treaty of 1819 had been something less than precise in their acquaintance with the geography of the Southwest and had overlooked the bifurcation of the Red River into a North Fork and a South Fork or Main Red River. The Texan commissioners insisted that the North Fork constituted the Red River within the meaning of the treaty of 1819; the commissioners of the United States insisted that the treaty contemplated the South Fork or Main Red River. It was after some decades of bickering that the United States finally decided to resort to an original proceeding in the Supreme Court to lay the controversy to rest.

Texas demurred to the bill, stressing three grounds. Although Article 3, Section 2, referred to controversies to which the United States shall be a party and to controversies between two or more states, nowhere did it refer to controversies between the United States and a state. It was not competent, Texas insisted, under the Constitution and laws of the United States of America, "for said United States of America to sue one of its component States in her own courts." In particular, there was no authority to institute such a suit in the Supreme Court within its original jurisdiction. Furthermore, Texas insisted, the United States was seeking a judicial decree to settle a question "which . . . is political in its nature and character and not susceptible of judicial determination by this court." The third ground was narrower, and I omit discussion of it here. (In its demurrer, Texas had cited also a fourth ground, which it abandoned in its argument.)

Texas pulled no punches in presenting its case. It insisted that the dispute could only be resolved by agreement between the United States and Texas. If no such agreement could be reached, "the result, according to the defendant's theory of the Constitution, must be that the United States . . . must bring its suit in one of the courts of Texas—that State consenting that its courts may be open for the assertion of claims against it by the United States—or that, in the end, there must be a trial of physical strength between the government of the Union and Texas."[13]

The first alternative, that the United States must sue in the courts of Texas, was held by the Supreme Court to be "unwarranted both by the letter and spirit of the Constitution." The second alternative—a trial of physical strength —"has no place in our constitutional system, and cannot be contemplated by any patriot except with feelings of deep concern."[14]

The court held that Article 3, Section 2, did encompass suits by the United States against a state and that the issues were not political but justiciable; and it decided them in favor of the United States.

The decision was handed down thirty-one years after Abraham Lincoln's message to the special session of Congress, but its logic would have been applicable in 1861. It does not follow that the Supreme Court in 1861 would have applied the same logic. That is another question. I turn for guidance to another case, growing out of the same boundary dispute, in another of its ramifications.

The bone of contention consisted of bonds issued in the partial settlement of 1850, previously mentioned, in which the United States agreed to pay Texas $10,000,000. The payment was made in five percent bearer bonds, of which $5,000,000 were delivered to Texas and $5,000,000 were retained in the national Treasury. By appropriate legislation, Texas provided that the bonds could be sold when duly endorsed by the governor of the state. Most were

---

13 United States v. Texas, 143 U.S. 621, 641, 12 S.Ct. 488, 492 (1892).
14 *Ibid.*

endorsed and sold according to the procedure described by law; and when the purchasers presented the bonds to the United States, they were paid. Part, however, were retained by the legislature of Texas as a school fund and remained in the state treasury until the outbreak of the Civil War.

In January 1861, sixty-one individuals, citizens of Texas, issued a call for a convention. In response to the call, delegates were elected from various sections of the state. The state legislature, convened in an extra session on January 22, 1861, ratified the election of the delegates to the convention. Assembling on February 1, the convention adopted an ordinance to dissolve the union between the state of Texas and the other states. The ordinance, subsequently submitted to the people, was adopted by a vote of 34,794 to 11,235. The convention thereupon reassembled, announced the count of the votes, and on March 4, declared Texas to have withdrawn from the Union of the United States. It passed a resolution requiring the officers of the state government to take an oath to support the provisional government of the Confederate States. When the governor of Texas and its secretary of state refused to take the oath, the convention declared them deposed. Under the authority of the rebel government, a number of the retained bonds in an aggregate amount of $125,000 were transferred to White and Childs, a commercial firm, in payment for a quantity of cotton cards and medicines.

After the defeat of the Confederacy, the President of the United States appointed a provisional governor for Texas, who arranged for the formation of a state government. Under his direction, the people adopted the new Constitution of 1866, under which a governor was elected. In 1867, Congress passed the first three of the five Reconstruction Acts. By the first, Texas and nine other named Southern states, as a group, were divided into five military districts. Texas and Louisiana constituted the fifth military district. The statute provided for the appointment of an army officer as a military governor for each of the five districts. His authority was plenary. When the people of any one of the states should have formed a new constitution, meeting requirements prescribed in the Reconstruction Act, notably agreement to the Fourteenth Amendment (after the Fourteenth Amendment should have become part of the Constitution of the United States), the state could have restored to it all of its rights and privileges under the Constitution. General Sheridan, the military governor for the fifth district, subsequently appointed a third governor of Texas.

It appeared that White and Childs and certain purchasers from them were seeking to present the bonds for payment by the United States. On February 15, 1867, the state of Texas sued in the Supreme Court to enjoin White and Childs and the others from obtaining payment, and to require them to surrender the bonds. In support of the suit, counsel exhibited letters of authorization from the provisional governor (Governor Hamilton) appointed by the President of the United States, the governor elected under the Constitution of 1866 (Governor Throckmorton), and the governor appointed by General Sheridan (Governor Pease). Counsel plainly foresaw attempted defenses based on a challenge to the authority of one or another of the governors. Their foresight was vindicated. Against a contention by the defendants that the persons filing the lawsuit did not represent the state of Texas, the Court held that "the suit was instituted and is prosecuted by competent authority."[15] But Messrs. White and Childs also invoked another defense full of implications for the present inquiry.

They challenged the right of an entity calling itself "Texas" to bring a lawsuit in the original jurisdiction of the Supreme Court. They insisted it was not a state. The Reconstruction Act of March 2, 1867, had consolidated Texas and Louisiana, as "rebel" states, into a fifth military district subject to the "military authority of the United States."[16] Although the legislation had provided a means by which Texas could be regenerated as a state, the conditions had not yet been satisfied. In consequence, the entity styling itself "Texas" had no standing in the Supreme Court. The argument persuaded three of the justices, who dissented.

Mr. Justice Grier, in dissenting, skirted a question concerning the constitutionality of the Reconstruction Act. In this, he was in accord with the majority. Chief Justice Salmon Chase, writing for the majority, took pains to note that "nothing in the case before us requires the court to pronounce judgment upon the constitutionality of any particular provision of these [the Reconstruction] acts."[17] Mr. Justice Grier also did "not consider [himself] bound to express any opinion judicially as to . . . the power of Congress to govern her [Texas] as a conquered province." For Grier,

---

[15] Texas v. White et al., 7 Wall. 700, 732, 19 Law. Ed. 227, 239 (1868).
[16] 14 Stat. 428.
[17] 7 Wall. 700, 731, 19 Law. Ed. 227, 239 (1868).

this might have created complications, since he intended to defer to a political judgment expressed in the statute. But he found his way through the confusion, explaining: "I can only submit to *the fact* as decided by the political position of the government; and I am not disposed to join in any essay to prove Texas to be a State of the Union, when Congress have decided that she is not. It is a question of fact, I repeat, and of fact only. *Politically,* Texas is not a *State in this Union.* Whether rightfully out of it or not is a question not before the court."[18]

The majority were not intimidated by the political implications. They faced the issue, held it to be justiciable, and decided it. Texas had been, at all times continued to be, and still remained a state. The conclusion was inescapable, for the "Constitution in all its provisions, looks to an indestructible Union, composed of indestructible States."[19] The words were uttered by Chief Justice Chase for the Supreme Court in 1868. They could have been spoken by Abraham Lincoln in 1861.

I return to the fantasy of a suit by the United States in the Supreme Court in 1861 against Georgia or Mississippi. The doctrines proclaimed by the Supreme Court in United States v. Texas in 1892 and in Texas v. White in 1868 established that the Supreme Court had jurisdiction over a dispute between the United States and a state; that the United States could institute a proceeding against a state in the original jurisdiction of the Supreme Court, and the Supreme Court could issue a decree against the defendant state; that a dispute over boundaries originally international was justiciable

---

18 7 Wall. 700, 739, 19 Law. Ed. 227, 242 (1868). (Italics in the original.)
19 7 Wall. 700, 725, 19 Law. Ed. 227, 237 (1868).

and not really political; and that questions of whether a state was indestructible and whether Texas was a state were justiciable and not merely political. By the same token, the Supreme Court would have had jurisdiction of a suit by the United States against Georgia or Mississippi in 1861. The question whether the Union was indestructible would have been no less justiciable and no more political than the question whether a state was indestructible. The principle that the Union was indestructible would have pointed unswervingly to a judgment that secession was unlawful. The Supreme Court could have issued a decree accordingly against Georgia or Mississippi. All this would have been and could have been *if* the Supreme Court in 1861 would have applied the logic of 1868 and 1892.

Why didn't Lincoln try it? For that matter, why didn't Georgia or Mississippi try it in reverse? Here again the possibilities are illuminated by later cases. In 1907, the Supreme Court distinguished a proceeding under Article 3, Section 2, by a state against the United States from a proceeding by the United States against a state. Neither case is covered explicitly by Article 3, Section 2. In the view of the Supreme Court, consent by a state to a suit against it by the United States "was given . . . when admitted into the Union."[20] But "it does not follow that because a State may be sued by the United States without its consent, therefore the United States may be sued by a State without its consent. Public policy forbids that conclusion."[21] The conclusion was reaffirmed in 1963.[22] It follows that *if* the Supreme Court in

<hr />

20 Kansas v. United States, 204 U.S. 331, 342, 27 S.Ct. 388, 391 (1906).
21 *Ibid.*
22 Hawaii v. Gordon, 373 U.S. 57, 83 S.Ct. 1052 (1963).

1861 would have applied the logic of the Court in 1907, Georgia or Mississippi could have sued the United States only with the latter's consent. If Georgia or Mississippi had taken the initiative to resolve the mortal issue of 1861 by adjudication, would Lincoln have consented? In either case, whether on the initiative of the United States or the initiative of a state with the consent of the United States, would the Supreme Court have exercised its jurisdiction and faced up to a decision?

We do not know and never can know. But there are clues to support a pretty good guess. In a passage from Lincoln's first inaugural address previously quoted, he revealed his conviction that the "people will have ceased to be their own rulers" if they were to leave "the policy of the government, upon vital questions affecting the whole people, . . . to be irrevocably fixed by decisions of the Supreme Court . . . in ordinary litigation between parties and personal actions." We can surmise that he would have adhered to his view even in relation to extraordinary litigation in which the parties would have been the United States Government and one or more states. He confronted an openly avowed purpose on the part of the dissident states to sever the Federal Union that left him "no choice . . . but to call out the war power of the government." The Southern states bluntly proclaimed that the American Union was secondary in importance to "the rights and principles" upon which they insisted and in behalf of which they were prepared to resist "even . . . to a disruption of every tie which binds [them] to the Union."[23] Since neither side would brook the possibility of an adverse

23 Milledgeville Resolution of 1850, see above, p. 11.

decision, neither would have invoked the jurisdiction of the Supreme Court unless it were certain of a judgment in its favor.

If either had instituted such a proceeding, there are other clues to warrant a guess as to how the Court would have responded. It may sharpen our conjectures if we first consider some hypothetical alternatives.

Assume a United States Constitution that explicitly affirmed the Union to be indestructible and indissoluble. It declared the adherence of the several states to be irrevocable and any purported withdrawal by a state to be void and of no effect. It expressly authorized and directed the Supreme Court to enjoin any attempt of a state to secede, upon a proper showing in a proceeding by the United States or any other state. Under such constitutional provisions, an exercise of jurisdiction by the Supreme Court in such a case would have entailed a minimal psychological burden for the members of the Court. In the minds of the judges, in the view of the society at large, in the view of the major political and social institutions of the society, and in the view of the other branches of government, the judges would have exercised no discretion but would have discharged a clear and unavoidable duty. In their minds and in the minds of the others, the judges would not have been personally accountable for the consequences.

Consider another hypothetical case. Assume a lawsuit in the Supreme Court governed by a broad and general constitutional or statutory provision. Assume also that the issues have only restricted implications. The passions of the litigants are not deeply engaged. Whatever the feelings involved, they are confined to the immediate litigants and a few others, with the society in general and its political and social institutions untouched. In such a case, a decision by the Court would involve a measure of judicial discretion, inescapable because of the breadth of the constitutional or statutory standard. But the society in general, its major political and social institutions, the other branches of government, and in most cases even the litigants themselves would feel they had a larger stake in a dependable procedure for an orderly and expeditious disposition of such controversies than in this or that outcome in the particular case. In deciding such a case, the judges would assume some burden of personal accountability for the consequences. For conscientious men, the burden is never negligible, but in the circumstances described, it would be readily bearable.

Although the two cases are imaginary, they reflect actual cases without number in the English and American legal systems and the civil law systems of Europe and Latin America. I offer some generalizations derived from them concerning the optimum conditions for adjudication. I speak of optimum, not necessary, conditions. Optimum, as here intended, does not mean calculated to elicit the highest expressions of the judicial art. It connotes circumstances in which judges find it easiest to decide and their decisions are most readily accepted by the parties and the community.

The optimum conditions are presented when the tribunal is long established in the regard of the people, who have seen it tested in a long and varied experience. The principles and standards to be applied by the tribunal in deciding the issues are accepted by the society in the sense that they emanate from established sources and through established procedures. The principles and standards for decisions have been established prior to the acts giving rise to the controversy. The principles and standards are precise and definite and are applied to the particular issue by an established method. To these must be added another set of factors, reflecting an interaction between the conditions for adjudication and the conditions for resort to adjudication by the parties to a controversy and for compliance with the resulting judgment.

The optimum conditions that foster a resort to adjudication by the parties embroiled in a dispute and compliance on their part with a judgment are presented when, in addition to the factors previously described, the issue has only restricted implications, and the consequences of a decision one way or the other are easy to foresee. The persons directly involved are few and only a very small fraction of the society identifies with them. To the society at large and its major social and political institutions—and even to the parties themselves—it is more important to sustain institutions for an orderly and expeditious disposition of such disputes than to arrive at this or that outcome in the particular dispute.

The conditions become progressively less favorable as the several factors move through the range of possible variations toward the other end of the spectrum. Adjudication is harder for a new and unfamiliar tribunal. It is harder even for an established tribunal if important segments of the society do not accept the principles and standards for decision or do not understand from what source or in what way the standards and principles were derived. It is harder even for an established tribunal applying accepted criteria, if the criteria are broad and vague.

Corresponding variations in the other factors have corresponding consequences. If the issues have far-reaching implications and the consequences of a judgment appear incalculable, the parties to a dispute will be less disposed to seek a judicial resolution. They will be still less inclined toward adjudication if a large part of the society is identified with each of the parties and major political or social institutions are involved. The disinclination will be intensified if emotions are so deeply engaged that a particular outcome may appear more important to the participants, and to large segments of the society and major political or social institutions identified with them, than the steady support of an institution for an orderly determination of disputes.

There comes a point in the spectrum where the limits of adjudication are reached, and the task becomes unmanageable. These are limits in an elemental sense, inherent in the nature of adjudication as exhibited by the historic experience of the great legal systems familiar to us. They lie beyond the limits that may be set for a particular court by a constitutional or statutory provision creating it. The elemental limits cannot be changed by a constitutional or statutory modification. They can be extended or contracted, if at all, only by alterations in political and legal concepts that would entail changes in the basic pattern of values, beliefs, and habits rooted in the culture and psychology of a people. If so profound a change did occur, it would engender philosophical disputes as to whether the modified process could still be properly regarded as adjudication. The dispute would be more than semantic. It would involve a question as to how far the historic experience of known legal systems could illuminate the prospects for the new process.

Wise and experienced judges do not ordinarily push the exercise of their functions up to the limits of adjudication. Their determination of where to impose self-restraint and draw the line will vary with their estimate of how the conditions are arrayed along the spectrum. It will also vary with their judicial philosophies.

These reflections naturally shape my conjectures concerning 1861. If a proceeding had been brought by the United States against Georgia or Mississippi in 1861, I believe the Court would have found the issues political and not justiciable. Even if the Court were composed of the same judges that issued the decree in United States v. Texas in 1892, they would have declined to exercise their jurisdiction in 1861. If, contrary to my conjecture, the Court would have decided the issues, its judgment would not have altered the event. The United States and the Confederacy would have gone to war. The judgment might not have been wholly without effect. One combatant might have been morally supported and the other morally hampered in "the opinion of mankind," to whatever degree and in whatever direction the judgment might have affected "the opinion of mankind."

These reflections, together with the hard evidence of what has actually happened, also shape my opinion concerning the relevance of international adjudication or quasi-adjudication to the settlement of Cold War disputes. To avoid misunderstanding, let me pause here to explain my terms and sound a warning.

"International adjudication and quasi-adjudication" are used here to comprehend adjudication in the precise legal sense; any decisions *ex aequo et bono* that may be attempted by the International Court of Justice pursuant to Article 38, Paragraph 2, of its Statute; arbitration within the meaning of Article 33, Paragraph 1, of the United Nations Charter that enjoins the parties to any dispute to "seek a solution by negotiation, enquiry, mediation, conciliation, *arbitration,* judicial settlement, resort to regional agencies or arrangements, or other peaceful means of their own choice" (italics mine); and any attempt at peaceful settlement through a resort to impartial third parties who may be authorized to use their own skill and discretion to try to work out an accommodation by fair and orderly procedures. "Cold War disputes" is a rough shorthand to encompass disputes involving American resistance to, or attempts to forestall, what the United States believes to be Soviet Russian or Communist Chinese expansionism. For the present inquiry, it is unnecessary to assess whether or how far American eyes that may see Soviet Russian or Chinese Communist aggression in any case may misread the evidence. It is also unnecessary to determine how far Soviet Russia's or Communist China's public description of the events in any case may conform to its private appraisal; or how far its private appraisal might fairly be regarded as supported by credible evidence. My focus is upon the relevance of international adjudication or quasi-adjudication to a peaceful settlement of a Cold War dispute after it has taken form.

I come to the warning note. When we undertake to bring

into focus the evidence, issues and choices involved in such a dispute, we encounter a pervasive hazard. The typical situation is many-faceted, intricate, and fluid, full of variations and intangibles. We seek to identify, sort out and describe the issues and choices and relate them to the evidence in a way to make them discussable, where the function of discussion is to arrive at a choice within the limits imposed by the practical possibilities of politics and law. In the very process of doing so, whatever the care exercised, we cannot avoid gliding over some of the intangibles and suppressing some of the subtleties. It is a price that must be paid to introduce a sufficient measure of clarity and definition to make the situation discussable in political and legal terms. But we must remain aware of the excluded subtleties and be ready to reintroduce them whenever the cost of continued exclusion becomes a loss of touch with reality.

If the states or international entities involved in an international Cold War dispute should want to undertake adjudication or quasi-adjudication, what tribunals might be available? There exist one standing court, the International Court of Justice, and at least two standing political entities, the Security Council of the United Nations and the Organ of Consultation of the Organization of American States. By agreement between the parties, judicial or arbitral tribunals can be created *ad hoc* for particular cases. In theory, there is also a possibility of creating new standing tribunals along lines envisaged by a number of imaginative writers. None of those that exist has the institutional status of a tribunal long known, long tested, and long secure in the regard of the people affected by its decisions. As to new entities that might be created, we cannot even speculate how long it might take them even to approximate such a status.

Taking the existing tribunals for what they are, what principles and criteria would they have available to reach a decision? In the case of the Security Council, the principles and standards can be found in Chapters I and VI of the United Nations Charter. They include the purpose of maintaining international peace and security; the prevention and removal of threats to the peace; the suppression of acts of aggression or other breaches of the peace; the adjustment of international disputes or situations that might lead to a breach of the peace; the bringing about of adjustments by peaceful means and in conformity with the principles of justice and international law; international cooperation; and the development of friendly relations among nations based on respect for the principles of equal rights and the self-determination of peoples. In the case of the Organ of Consultation of the Organization of American States, they include the obligation of the member states to cooperate with one another in a broad spirit of good neighborliness; protection of the peace of the Americas; respect for the fundamental rights and duties of states; and an obligation to use peaceful procedures to settle international disputes. In essence, these boil down to a single general principle or standard, the concept of peaceful settlement itself. In the case of the International Court of Justice, the criteria are the familiar terms of Article 38 of the Statute: international conventions; international custom as evidence of a general practice accepted as law; the general principles of law recognized by civilized nations; and, in Paragraph 2, not yet used, the principle of *ex aequo et bono.*

The parties to Cold War disputes are great states, the major political and social entities of contemporary international life, unrivaled for international power and status by any other existing organization except perhaps for the great organized religions.

In Cold War disputes, the issues typically fall into the categories described in standard diplomatic parlance as "vital." If the vital character sometimes seems to lie in the eye of the beholder, that does not necessarily make it any less real in terms of human behavior. There is no need to remind ourselves how tiny and remote corners of the earth's surface, or even more remote sectors of outer space, can become identified in the minds of governments with survival, independence, and honor.

The art of diplomacy has long recognized that one of the most hopeful methods for seeking a peaceful settlement is to reshape the issues to squeeze the significance out of them. But as long as the issues remain charged with deep implications, they tend to be intractable.

In sum, in international Cold War disputes, the conditions for adjudication or quasi-adjudication at best lie at the far edge of the spectrum. Typically, they lie beyond the limits.

The factors that may place a dispute beyond the limits of adjudication (or quasi-adjudication) may also impair the possibility for negotiation, in the sense of discussion seeking a mutual accommodation through an emphasis upon common interests and common purposes. In circumstances when principles and criteria for adjudication or quasi-adjudication cannot be formulated, it is likely to be difficult to find common interests and common purposes. In such a case, it may be necessary to shift the search for accommodation toward a give-and-take in which estimates of probable gain are measured against estimates of probable loss under varying assumptions. I assume that this is what Winston Churchill may have had in mind when he said, "We cannot negotiate with the Russians, but we can bargain with them."

My conclusion about the limits of adjudication or quasi-adjudication need not drive us to despair for peace, nor to a loss of regard for the role of adjudication. Adjudication remains among the great institutional achievements of mankind. Like all human creations, it has its appropriate sphere. Its particular forms and applications can be increased, and it may have unrealized potentialities to be fulfilled, but there are limits even to its potential scope. Although striving in each generation to maximize its use in accordance with its nature, we must take care not to dissipate the precious resource by wishful misapplications. If my conclusion is well founded, it should drive us into a search for other, more pertinent ways and means to curb international disputes of a Cold War type and to steer them toward an outcome that is peaceful or at least not destructive. In the final chapter of this book, I shall suggest an attitude and pattern of behavior that might improve the prospects in such a search. At this point, I turn to consider disputes of another kind.

CHAPTER THREE

DISPUTES BETWEEN

NON-SELF-GOVERNING PEOPLES

AND ESTABLISHED STATES

Under traditional doctrine, adjudication and quasi-adjudication[1] under international law appear to have even less relevance to disputes between modern industrial states administering "territories whose peoples have not yet attained a full measure of self-government" and the "inhabitants of these territories"[2] than to Cold War controversies. International law contains doctrines that bear upon Cold War conflicts, notably in regard to territory, boundaries, sovereignty, aggression, and self-defense. These doctrines often play a part in the setting for Cold War disputes, although such disputes typically lie beyond the reach of adjudication or quasi-adjudication. But at least until the end of World War I, neither customary international law nor the concepts derived from treaties had any significant bearing upon controversies between colonial peoples (as non-self-governing peoples were then known) and colonial powers. The familiar international law doctrine pointed quite the other way. Under it, such controversies were "internal" and "domes-

---

1 As defined in Chapter 2, p. 36.
2 See United Nations Charter, Art. 73.

tic." As such, they lay beyond the competence of any international legal authority and beyond the cognizance of substantive international law.

The traditional doctrine was modified along the edges by the system of mandates inaugurated by the treaties following World War I. A new and radical notion pushed its head above the soil. As it emerged, it related only to former colonies or former territory of Germany and Turkey, defeated in World War I. The famous Article 22 of the Covenant of the League of Nations gave voice to the new idea in its opening paragraphs:

> 1. To those colonies and territories which as a consequence of the late war have ceased to be under the sovereignty of the States which formerly governed them and which are inhabited by peoples not yet able to stand by themselves under the strenuous conditions of the modern world, there should be applied the principle that the well-being and development of such peoples form a sacred trust of civilization and that securities for the performance of this trust should be embodied in this Covenant.
>
> 2. The best method of giving practical effect to this principle is that the tutelage of such peoples should be entrusted to advanced nations who by reason of their resources, their experience or their geographical position can best undertake this responsibility, and who are willing to accept it, and that this tutelage should be exercised by them as Mandatories on behalf of the League.[3]

3 From the text, signed June 28, 1919, in force January 10, 1920, published by the Secretariat of the League, conveniently available in *International*

Article 22 classified the new mandates into three groups. One, informally designated Class A, comprised communities that had "reached a stage of development where their existence as independent nations can be provisionally recognized subject to the rendering of administrative advice and assistance by a Mandatory until such time as they are able to stand alone." A second, called Class B, included other peoples, "especially those of Central Africa," who were "at such a stage that the Mandatory must be responsible for the administration of the territory under conditions which will guarantee freedom of conscience and religion, subject only to the maintenance of public order and morals, the prohibition of abuses such as the slave trade, the arms traffic and the liquor traffic and the prevention of the establishment of fortifications or military and naval bases and of military training of the natives for other than police purposes and the defense of territory." The third, Class C, comprehended territories "such as South-West Africa and certain of the South Pacific Islands, which, owing to the sparseness of their population, or their small size, or their remoteness from the centres of civilization, or their geographical contiguity to the territory of the Mandatory . . . can be best administered under the laws of the Mandatory as integral portions of its territory, subject to the safeguards above mentioned in the interests of the indigenous population." By Paragraph 7 of Article 22, the Mandatory in the case of every mandate was required to "render to the Council [of the League] an annual report in reference to the territory committed to its charge." In each case, the degree of authority to be exercised

---

Legislation, ed. Manley O. Hudson (Washington, D. C.: Carnegie Endowment for International Peace, 1931), I, 13.

by the Mandatory was to be explicitly defined by the Council of the League.

The new political and legal idea was rooted in an old morality and system of values. If I may quote from a book of my own:

> . . . while the twin drives to establish independent states and to modernize underdeveloped societies reached a peak of intensity in the aftermath of World War II, their origins can be traced back to the expansion of Europe and to the Industrial Revolution, the French Revolution, and the American Revolution.
>
> The science and technology that transformed Europe and North America spread to the other continents along the highways of exploration, trade, conquest and colonization. So did the ideas proclaimed in the Declaration of Independence and the Declaration of the Rights of Man. As the strength of the West reduced areas to a colonial condition or other forms of dependence, the culture of the West planted seeds in those areas that sprouted ultimately in aspirations toward self-fulfillment and a will to emulate Western productivity and power. Lumumba and Kasavubu in the Republic of the Congo in 1960 were would-be heirs, presumably unknowing, of Jefferson and Danton as well as of unnumbered scientists and inventors of whom they had never heard. Yet, as they discovered, a claim to a heritage and even its allowance do not automatically lead to an enjoyment of its benefits. There must be an understanding of the heritage and a capacity to put it to use.[4]

4 Milton Katz, *The Things That Are Caesar's* (New York: Alfred A. Knopf, Inc., 1966), p. 44.

After World War II, the Charter of the United Nations nourished the growth of the idea. Chapter XI, consisting of Articles 73 and 74, and Chapter XII, embracing Articles 75 to 85, contain the core of the newer elements of the new doctrine.

Chapter XII established an international trusteeship system. The system applied to "such territories as may be placed thereunder by subsequent individual agreements." Its basic objectives were "to further international peace and security" and "to promote the political, economic, social and educational advancement of the inhabitants of the trust territories, and their progressive development towards self-government or independence as may be appropriate to the particular circumstances of each territory and its peoples and the freely expressed wishes of the peoples concerned." Territories to be comprehended within the trusteeship system would be placed under a trustee through trusteeship agreements. Such agreements could be effected for territories falling into any one of three specified groups: "territories now held under mandate"; "territories . . . detached from enemy states as the result of the Second World War"; and "territories voluntarily placed under the system by states responsible for their administration." The terms of each trusteeship were to be determined by agreement between the states directly concerned, "including the mandatory power in the case of territories held under mandate by a Member of the United Nations."

Article 80 reveals on its face the tensions of a compromise between states seeking the prompt termination of World War I mandates in favor of new trusteeship agreements and states insistent on preserving the rights of mandatory powers under the mandate agreements. Paragraph 1 of Article 80 makes explicit that "nothing in this Chapter shall be construed in or of itself to alter in any manner the rights whatsoever of any states or any peoples or the terms of existing international instruments to which Members of the United Nations may . . . be parties"; but Paragraph 2 emphasizes that Paragraph 1 is not to "be interpreted as giving grounds for delay or postponement of the negotiation and conclusion of agreements for placing mandated and other territories under the trusteeship system."

It is Chapter XI, entitled Declaration Regarding Non-Self-Governing Territories, that is perhaps the most revolutionary component of contemporary international law in regard to non-self-governing peoples. Articles 73 and 74 provide:

Article 73

Members of the United Nations which have or assume responsibilities for the administration of territories whose peoples have not yet attained a full measure of self-government recognize the principle that the interests of the inhabitants of these territories are paramount, and accept as a sacred trust the obligation to promote to the utmost, within the system of international peace and security established by the present Charter, the well-being of the inhabitants of these territories, and, to this end:

a. to ensure, with due respect for the culture of the peoples concerned, their political, economic, social, and educational advancement, their just treatment, and their protection against abuses;

b. to develop self-government, to take due account of the political aspirations of the peoples, and to assist them in the progressive development of their free political institutions, according to the particular circumstances of each territory and its peoples and their varying stages of advancement;

c. to further international peace and security;

d. to promote constructive measures of development, to encourage research, and to cooperate with one another and, when and where appropriate, with specialized international bodies with a view to the practical achievement of the social, economic, and scientific purposes set forth in this Article; and

e. to transmit regularly to the Secretary-General for information purposes, subject to such limitation as security and constitutional considerations may require, statistical and other information of a technical nature relating to economic, social, and educational conditions in the territories for which they are respectively responsible other than those territories to which Chapter XII and XIII apply.

Article 74

Members of the United Nations also agree that their policy in respect of the territories to which this Chapter applies, no less than in respect of their metropolitan areas, must be based on the general principle of good-neighborliness, due account being taken of the interests and well-being of the rest of the world, in social, economic, and commercial matters.

By these articles, members of the United Nations administering "non-self-governing territories" expressly accept what are expressly described as obligations. Are these legal obligations? If not, what sort of obligations are they? If they are legal obligations, are they enforceable by proceedings in the International Court of Justice between member states that have accepted the jurisdiction of the Court?

To laymen and to lawyers other than international lawyers, it may be surprising that the questions should be asked. The Charter of the United Nations is a treaty. It is elementary learning that treaties "are agreements, of a contractual character, between States, or organizations of States, creating legal rights and obligations between the Parties."[5] The contracting parties are "bound by its provisions, and . . . they must execute it in all its parts."[6] Should it not follow as a matter of course that the "obligations" of Article 73 are obligations binding in law? It may follow, but not as a matter of course and not in a straight line, and not necessarily in all cases. I pause to sort out cases and meanings. To do so, it will be necessary to take an exploratory detour.

There are treaties and treaties. A publication entitled "Treaties in Force," compiled by the Office of the Legal Adviser of the Department of State, lists treaties in effect to which the United States is a party. Each treaty is identified

---

[5] L. Oppenheim, *International Law*, 8th ed. H. Lauterpacht (London, New York, and Toronto: Longmans, Green & Co., 1955), I, 877.
[6] *Ibid.*, p. 923.

by its title, the date and place of signature, the date of entry into force, the citation in U. S. Statutes at Large, and the citation in one of the standard treaty series. That is all. The bare listing covers 296 pages, each divided into two columns. The subjects are as varied as international life. They range from a convention between the United States and the United Kingdom relating to the tenure and disposition of real and personal property to an agreement between the United States and Dahomey relating to economic and technical assistance; from a treaty between the United States and Denmark establishing reciprocal treatment for passenger motor vehicles to a treaty between the United States and Czechoslovakia for the mutual extradition of fugitive criminals; from a parcel-post agreement between the United States and Colombia to a treaty with Canada for the avoidance of double taxation on incomes and the prevention of income-tax evasion to a treaty between the United States and Costa Rica concerning the construction of an inter-American highway within the borders of Costa Rica; from an agreement between the United States and Ecuador for the financing of educational exchange programs to an agreement between the United States and the Federal Republic of Germany establishing procedures for the reciprocal filing of classified patent applications; from a treaty among the United States, the United Kingdom, and Ghana relating to pilot licenses for civil aircraft to a copyright treaty between the United States and India; from a treaty establishing the International Atomic Energy Agency to the Inter-American Treaty for Reciprocal Assistance; from the North Atlantic Treaty to the Charter of the United Nations.

The variety of approaches and meanings matches the range of titles and subjects. Consider and compare two examples.

An Air Transport Services agreement between the United States and France, effective March 27, 1946, established routes to be served by the air carriers of each that involved points of departure, destination, or overflight in the territory of the other. Schedule II, listing routes to be served by American air carriers, included one described as follows: "1. The United States via intermediate points over the North Atlantic to Paris and beyond via intermediate points in Switzerland, Italy, Greece, Egypt, *the Near East,* India, Burma and Siam to Hanoi, and thence to China and beyond; in both directions"[7] (italics mine). In 1955, Pan American Airways notified the American and French governments that it intended to begin operations to Turkey on a route through Paris and Rome to Istanbul. The civil aviation authorities of France promptly objected, on the ground that Istanbul was located in Europe rather than in "the Near East" and therefore fell outside the scope of the authorized route. The issue was limited and specific. Did the term "Near East" in Route 1 of Schedule II cover Istanbul in Turkey? When the governments found themselves unable to resolve the issue through negotiation, they referred it to arbitration pursuant to Article X of the treaty, as amended.[8] The arbitral tribunal consisted of three lawyers, one selected by each contracting party and the third named by the President of the International Court of Justice on default of an

---

7 TIAS 1679, p. 26 (March 27, 1946); 139 UNTS 114, 136.
8 TIAS 2257, pp. 3-4 (March 19, 1951); 139 UNTS 151, 154.

agreed choice by the first two. Each state was represented by counsel, and the proceedings consisted of written pleadings and oral hearings. The issues, the procedure and the patterns of argument and decision were "legal."

It is hardly necessary to mention that "law" and "legal" have many meanings. In the present context, I employ these terms in a workaday sense, as practicing lawyers in the United States, Britain, or continental Europe would employ "law" and "legal" in the course of their practice. In this usage, the terms signify the kinds of doctrine and methods that are regularly applied by lawyers and judges in the common law and civil law systems to the kinds of problems that regularly come to them for treatment. "Legal" and "law" connote the characteristic patterns of thought and analysis of such lawyers acting in their professional capacity and the spheres of their acknowledged expertise.

I turn from the foregoing actual case to a hypothetical case that conceivably could arise under the North Atlantic Treaty:[9] Under Article 5 of the treaty, the parties "agree that an armed attack against one or more of them in Europe or North America shall be considered an attack against them all; and consequently they agree that, if such an armed attack occurs, each of them . . . will assist the Party or Parties so attacked by taking forthwith, individually and in concert with the other Parties, such action as it deems necessary, including the use of armed force, to restore and maintain the security of the North Atlantic area." Article 6 clarifies the meaning of "an armed attack . . . in Europe or North America" by stipulating that the protected area in-

[9] TIAS 1964 (Aug. 24, 1949), 34 UNTS 243.

cludes "the territory of any of the Parties in Europe or North America, . . . the Algerian Departments of France, . . . the occupation forces of any Party in Europe, . . . the islands under the jurisdiction of any Party in the North Atlantic area north of the Tropic of Cancer or . . . the vessels or aircraft in this area of any of the Parties."

Suppose that a NATO state—say France, perhaps, or Greece—should announce itself the victim of an armed attack on its vessels or aircraft in the Mediterranean Sea at a distance of some fifty miles from the coast of Egypt or Lybia and should invoke the assistance of its allies. Suppose that the alleged attacking state proclaimed that it had acted in self-defense against an aggressive move. To determine its obligations under the treaty, the United States (or any other NATO state) would have to determine whether the incident involved "an armed attack" within the meaning of Article 5; whether the events occurred "in Europe or North America" within the meaning of Article 5 and Article 6; and what action the United States (or such other NATO state) deemed necessary "to restore and maintain the security of the North Atlantic area," again within the meaning of Article 5. It is easy to imagine tense deliberations in Washington, under insistent demands from Paris or Athens, as the case might be. It is by no means easy to imagine a reference of such a situation to an arbitral tribunal composed of lawyers, who would be requested to resolve the issues upon due consideration of written pleadings and oral argument presented by counsel representing the several states. It seems in fact probable that no such reference would occur. Elements of legal analysis would have their place in the deliberations in Washington, and the Attorney General and the Legal Adviser of the Department of State might well be consulted. But we may predict that the fundamental and controlling process of thought would not be juridical.

We are left with a question whether the dominant process of thought ought to be juridical. How far should a requirement of objective legal analysis as the established means to determine the rights and duties of the parties be deemed to be incorporated in such an instrument as the North Atlantic Treaty?

In NATO, the participating states embarked upon far-reaching political and military engagements over a period of years. At no point does the treaty purport to define or touch the rights, duties, or expectations of private individuals or enterprises. The treaty involves a political and strategic assessment of the needs and expectations of great states, and it projects their individual and joint estimates and plans. When such a treaty is negotiated and signed, none of the participating states contemplates that its future course under the treaty will be governed exclusively or primarily by technical juridical procedures or patterns of analysis. No participating state considers itself to have acquired a right to demand that the course of conduct of the other participating states should be so determined. The relevant procedures are diplomatic, and the relevant intellectual canons are the canons of political thought—with something added. The addition is a sense of law. In the language of lawyers, Article 5 of the North Atlantic Treaty constitutes a formal statement of policy, a formal declaration of purpose or declaration of intent, upon which the participating states are entitled reciprocally to rely subject to the limitations inherent in the nature of such a declaration. Article 5 neither expresses nor was intended to express a contractual obligation in the strict legal sense. It does nevertheless express an obligation. The obligation is diplomatic, reinforced by what I call a sense of law. In speaking of a "sense of law," I acknowledge the hazard that I may be unconsciously seeking to cover an absence of rational or practical meaning by an elegant phrase. Let me test it in relation to our suppositious case under Article 5 and Article 6 of the North Atlantic Treaty.

I have ventured an opinion that, under Articles 5 and 6 properly understood, the choices open to the President and his advisers would not be and should not be confined within the limits that would be imposed by a rigorous and objective technical legal analysis. Does it follow that the President and his Cabinet would and should feel free to reach whatever choice their current political estimates and practical preferences might suggest? I do not think so. The words of the treaty should impose a constraint, and would do so. The President would be guided by his assessment of the immediate and long-range national needs, interests, and purposes of the United States. But I believe that a sense of a commitment by the United States and of a right of reliance by the others under the treaty would enter into his assessment, and that elements of legal analysis would play a part along with other modes of thought. The extent to which this happened would determine the operational meaning of "diplomatic obligation reinforced by a sense of law" in the particular case. The meaning of a "sense of law" in other cases will be explored in a subsequent chapter, along with a question of whether and how it may differ from a sense of honor or a sense of morality.

The Air Transport Services Agreement of March 27, 1946, between the United States and France and the North Atlantic Treaty are limiting cases, lying at opposite edges of a broad range of graduated variations. More precisely, it is Route 1 of Schedule II of the Air Transport Services Agreement of March 27, 1946, and Article 5 of the North Atlantic Treaty that are the limiting cases. It is not only treaties, but particular provisions of particular treaties, that lie at different points along the range of gradations.

It may help put these matters in perspective to recall the differentiations among types of contracts in domestic law and among types of provisions in contracts. Although an agreement to sell a tract of land, an installment sales contract for an automobile, a life insurance policy, a collective bargaining agreement between a union and an employer, a partnership among investment bankers or lawyers, a charter of a corporation, and a marriage are all classified as "contracts," no experienced lawyer or businessman imagines them to be identical in their operation or consequences. The standard curricula of law schools bear eloquent testimony to the weight of the differences. The law of commercial contracts is ordinarily taught in a course named Contracts; but the law of labor agreements typically is taught in a course named Labor Law, the law of insurance policies in a course named Insurance, the law of partnership agreements in a course named Partnership, the law of corporations in a course named Corporations or Business Organizations, and the law affecting marriage contracts in a course called Domestic Relations or Family Law. It is the distinctive attributes of the several varieties that are emphasized rather than their common exemplification of the institution of contract.

Within marriage contracts and partnership agreements, there lie obligations that sound in morality, honor, or good taste rather than in law. Many are implicit. Some, like the promise to "love, honor and cherish" are explicit. They involve reciprocal commitments and rights of reliance and not infrequently go to the heart of the relationship. But their metes and bounds are not traced by legal analysis, nor do controversies that involve them respond to treatment through legal procedures.

To return to Chapter XI of the Charter: A glance at its terms reveals the variety in the scope of the "obligations" that are "accepted" by member states administering non-self-governing territories. Paragraph e of Article 73 is comparatively precise and limited. It requires member states "to transmit regularly to the Secretary-General for information purposes . . . statistical and other information of a technical nature relating to economic, social, and educational conditions in the territories for which they are respectively responsible . . ." But even this requirement is qualified by an express stipulation making it "subject to such limitations as security and constitutional considerations may require." It is a far cry from paragraph e to paragraph b of Article 73, and an even farther cry to paragraph c. Under paragraph b, the member state acknowledges its duty "to develop self-government, to take due account of the political aspirations of the peoples, and to assist them in the progressive development of their free political institutions, according to the particular circumstances of each territory and its peoples and their varying stages of advancement." Under paragraph c, the member state undertakes to "further international peace and security." How far do the several paragraphs state undertakings in a legal sense, and how far in a political? By what authority and by what procedures are their meanings and their consequences to be ascertained?

At the end of 1955, the General Assembly and the Secretary General began a new phase in probing the reach of Article 73 of the Charter. For the first time, they tested the scope of the most nearly specific of its provisions, paragraph e, against a state candidly hostile to the entire Article.[10] The occasion was the entry of Portugal into the United Nations.

Portugal, least sensitive among West European colonial powers to the winds of change, entered the United Nations in December 1955, when the logjam in admissions to membership broke to admit a growing complement of Asian and African states. Resisting new arrangements, Portugal had not entirely disregarded the importance of a "new look." In 1951, it had revised its constitution to rename its overseas territories, which were represented to the world as "provinces" of metropolitan Portugal. Unimpressed by the new nomenclature, the Secretary General of the United Nations included Portugal among the members to which he sent notes requesting reports under Chapter XI of the Charter

---

10 For earlier examples of the application of Article 73, paragraph e, see UN Yearbook, 1948-1949, pp. 730-734 (cessation of the transmission of information voluntarily transmitted).

concerning their "non-self-governing" territories. Portugal blandly explained that it administered no territory falling within Chapter XI. Pointing to its revised constitution, Portugal explained that its provinces, whether within metropolitan Portugal or overseas, constituted inseparable parts of a unitary state.

The African and Asian members of the U.N. were not persuaded. In the Eleventh General Assembly (1956), they opened a campaign to define the rights of non-self-governing territories and the duties of states that had "responsibilities for the administration" of such territories. The campaign swelled as the Asian and African membership of the United Nations grew. When the Fifteenth General Assembly convened, the Asian and African states raised the campaign to a pitch of intensity that has been sustained ever since.

On December 14, 1960, the Fifteenth General Assembly adopted its famous Resolution No. 1514 (XV), a "Declaration on the Granting of Independence to Colonial Countries and Peoples." Recognizing the "passionate yearning for freedom in all dependent peoples" and the "increasing conflicts resulting from the denial of or impediments in the way of the freedom of such peoples, which constitute a serious threat to world peace," insisting that "the process of liberation is irresistible and irreversible and that, in order to avoid serious crises, an end must be put to colonialism and all practices of segregation and discrimination associated therewith," Resolution No. 1514 (XV) declared that:

1. The subjection of peoples to alien subjugation, domination and exploitation constitutes a denial of

fundamental human rights, is contrary to the Charter of the United Nations and is an impediment to the promotion of world peace and cooperation;

2. All peoples have the right to self-determination; by virtue of that right they freely determine their political status and freely pursue their economic, social and cultural development;

3. Inadequacy of political, economic, social or educational preparedness should never serve as a pretext for delaying of independence; ...

5. Immediate steps shall be taken, in Trust and Non-Self-Governing Territories or all other territories which have not yet attained independence, to transfer all powers to the peoples of those territories, without any conditions or reservations, in accordance with their freely expressed will and desire, without any distinction as to race, creed or colour, in order to enable them to enjoy complete independence and freedom.[11]

The day after the adoption of Resolution No. 1514 (XV), the General Assembly voted Resolutions No. 1541 and 1542, defining the principles by which members of the United Nations would determine whether obligations existed to transmit reports concerning non-self-governing territories under paragraph e of Chapter XI of the Charter. Less than a year later, on November 27, 1961, the General Assembly added Resolution No. 1654 (XVI), establishing a committee of seventeen members, to be known as the Special Committee on the Situation with Regard to the Implementation of

11 Gen. Ass. Res. 1514 (XV) (Dec. 14, 1960), U.N. Gen. Ass. Off. Rec. 15th Sess., Annexes (Agenda Item 87), p. 8.

the Declaration on the Granting of Independence to Colonial Countries and Peoples. Charged with responsibility for giving effect to Resolution No. 1514 (XV), the Special Committee became the symbol and the center of General Assembly effort to promote independent statehood for non-self-governing peoples. After a little more than a year, the Special Committee was enlarged to a membership of twenty-four, by Resolution No. 1810 (XVII) of December 17, 1962. The United States has been a member of this Special Committee from the beginning.

Resolution No. 1810 (XVII) went beyond mere changes in organization. Noting with "profound regret" that Resolution No. 1514 had not been "fully implemented in a large number of territories and that, in certain cases, even preliminary measures have not yet been taken to realize its objectives," and deeply concerned by "the negative attitude and the deliberate refusal of certain administering Powers to cooperate with the Special Committee," the Resolution urged all "administering Powers to take immediate steps in order that all colonial territories and peoples may accede to independence without delay." It charged the enlarged Special Committee with a duty of continuing "to seek the most suitable ways and means for the speedy and total application of the Declaration to all territories which have not yet attained independence."[12]

A year later, on December 11, 1963, the Security Council added the weight of its opinion to the General Assembly's views on self-determination. Recalling its own Resolution

[12] Gen. Ass. Res. 1810 (XVII) (Dec. 17, 1962), U.N. Gen. Ass. Off. Rec. 17th Sess., Annexes, I (Agenda Item 25), p. 7.

No. 180 of July 31, 1963, in which it had proclaimed the situation in Angola a danger to the maintenance of international peace and security, the Security Council, in Resolution No. 183, expressly reaffirmed "the interpretation of self-determination laid down in General Assembly Resolution 1514 (XV) as follows: "All peoples have the right to self-determination; by virtue of that right they freely determine their political status and freely pursue their economic, social and cultural development."[13]

Thus in the sequence of resolutions, focused upon Angola as a test case, the embattled Committee of Twenty-four, abetted by the Asian and African membership of the United Nations, moved the General Assembly and the Security Council to forcible declarations concerning the scope and meaning of Article 73. Angola was by no means the only test case. The Territory of South West Africa was another, longer standing than Angola, and Southern Rhodesia still another. They led to comparable pronouncements.

The declarations sounded loud and clear in political terms. At least they were clear up to a point. They expressed the political attitude of a majority of the General Assembly and a minimum of seven of the eleven members of the Security Council, including the permanent members. Subsequent events would tell how far the political attitude might be given effect in political action designed to make the resolutions stick. However clear the political attitude and whatever the outcome might be in political action, questions remained concerning the legal significance of the resolutions.

---

[13] Sec. Council Res. 183 (Dec. 11, 1963), Sec. Council Off. Rec. 18th year, Supp. for Oct., Nov., Dec. (S/5481), pp. 110-111.

Could the resolutions determine how far the undertakings in Article 73 constituted contractual commitments rather than declarations of intention? Could they authoritatively interpret the several provisions? Their authority to do so has been questioned. The questions are not without support in the terms of the Charter and its legislative history.

At the San Francisco Conference from which the Charter of the United Nations emerged in 1945, a question "How and by what organ or organs of the Organization should the Charter be interpreted?" had been submitted to Committee 2 (Legal Problems) of Commission IV (Judicial Organization). Committee 2's reply stated the view that prevailed at the Conference:

> In the course of the operations from day to day of the various organs of the Organization, it is inevitable that each organ will interpret such parts of the Charter as are applicable to its particular functions. This process is inherent in the functioning of any body which operates under an instrument defining its functions and powers. It will be manifested in the functioning of such a body as the General Assembly, the Security Council, or the International Court of Justice. Accordingly, it is not necessary to include in the Charter a provision either authorizing or approving the normal operation of this principle.
>
> Difficulties may conceivably arise in the event that there should be a difference of opinion among the organs of the Organization concerning the correct interpretation of a provision of the Charter. Thus, two or-

gans may conceivably hold and may express or even act upon different views. Under unitary forms of national government the final determination of such a question may be vested in the highest court or in some other national authority. However, the nature of the Organization and of its operation would not seem to be such as to invite the inclusion in the Charter of any provision of this nature. If two member states are at variance concerning the correct interpretation of the Charter, they are of course free to submit the dispute to the International Court of Justice as in the case of any other treaty. Similarly, it would always be open to the General Assembly or to the Security Council, in appropriate circumstances, to ask the International Court of Justice for an advisory opinion concerning the meaning of a provision of the Charter. Should the General Assembly or the Security Council prefer another course, an *ad hoc* committee of jurists might be set up to examine the question and report its views, or recourse might be had to a joint conference . . .

It is to be understood, of course, that if an interpretation made by any organ of the Organization or by a committee of jurists is not generally acceptable it will be without binding force. In such circumstances, or in cases where it is desired to establish an authoritative interpretation as a precedent for the future, it may be necessary to embody the interpretation in an amendment to the Charter.[14]

14 UNCIO Doc. 933, IV/2/42/(2), p. 8; 13 UNCIO Doc., p. 709; see also U.N. Doc. A/474, Nov. 13, 1947.

As late as July 20, 1962, the International Court of Justice accepted the opinion expressed by Committee 2 of Commission IV in 1945 as still valid. In its Advisory Opinion on Expenses of the United Nations, the Court acknowledged that "Proposals made during the drafting of the Charter to place the ultimate authority to interpret the Charter in the International Court of Justice were not accepted . . . As anticipated in 1945, therefore, each organ must, in the first place at least, determine its own jurisdiction."[15]

Suppose that the General Assembly or the Security Council should request an advisory opinion of the International Court of Justice on whether paragraph b of Article 73 requires Portugal to grant self-government to the non-self-governing people of Portuguese Angola. Suppose further that the Court should render an opinion in accord with the views previously stated of the General Assembly and the Security Council? Would Portugal be legally bound? Would any other state be legally bound?

Under Article 96 of the Charter, the General Assembly or the Security Council may request the International Court of Justice for an advisory opinion on any legal question. But nothing in the Charter or the Statute of the International Court of Justice requires the General Assembly or the Security Council, as the case may be, to accept such an advisory opinion when given. When a request for an advisory opinion has been made, interested states may appear before the Court. But nothing in the Charter or the Statute of the Court indicates that a state so appearing will be bound by the advisory opinion. An inference to the contrary can be

15 ICJ Rep. 1962, pp. 151, 168 (July 20, 1962).

drawn from Article 59 of the Statute of the Court, relating
to contentious proceedings, which provides that the "decision of the Court has no binding force except between the
parties and in respect of that particular case." Such an inference has in fact been drawn by more than one commentator,
not only from Article 59 of the Statute of the Court, but
from the terms of the Charter and the Statute as a whole,
and from a concept of the nature of international law.

I am aware that this analysis may appear traumatic to
domestic lawyers and thoughtful laymen. If an advisory
opinion of the International Court of Justice is not binding
upon the General Assembly or Security Council that requested it, what function does it serve? If even an acceptance
of an advisory opinion by the General Assembly or the Security Council does not bind dissident member states, where
are we? If power resides nowhere to interpret the Charter
definitively, is the Charter a regime of law? These questions
have traumatized more than one international lawyer, strug-
gling to escape from the implications of the analysis that
underlies them. Judge Phillip Jessup, dissenting in the
South West Africa Cases, Second Phase, offers the following
comfort:

> Although an Advisory Opinion or a series of such opin-
> ions, is not or are not legally binding on a State Mem-
> ber of the United Nations, whether or not the opinion
> is accepted and endorsed by the General Assembly, I
> share the view stated by Judge John Bassett Moore and
> recalled with approval by Judge Winiarski in his dis-
> senting opinion in *Peace Treaties* (ICJ Reports 1950,
> pp. 89 and 91): "If the opinions are treated as mere

utterances and freely discarded, they will inevitably bring the Court into disrepute: . . . the Court must, in view of its high mission, attribute to them great legal value and a moral authority."

So Judge Azevedo in the same case said that although an ordinary advisory opinion did not produce the effects of *res judicata*, "that fact is not sufficient to deprive an advisory opinion of all the moral consequences which are inherent in the dignity of the organ delivering the opinion, or even of its legal consequences."[16]

In the context of the South West Africa Cases, Second Phase, Judge Jessup's observation carried a punch. When transferred to the context of our present analysis, it does little to relieve our discomfort. I turn to another seasoned and learned commentator:

> With respect to the general problem of the role of law in the United Nations, some theoretical observations may be made. It has been argued that the United Nations is essentially a political and dynamic institution . . . To this writer such a view is not persuasive. There is no contradiction between the essentially political character of the United Nations as an international institution and its obligation to respect applicable rules . . .
>
> The United Nations is indeed a political and dynamic institution, but it does not follow, as sometimes suggested, that it operates in a politico-legal vacuum. Politically it operates within the system of sovereign

16 ICJ Rep. 1966, pp. 6, 338 (July 18, 1966).

states competing and cooperating; legally it operates within the framework of the Charter . . . It should not be forgotten, however, that the often quoted San Francisco statement on interpretation . . . says: [here the author quotes the opinion of Committee 2 of Commission IV].

. . . As a consequence, it follows as a working rule that for an interpretation to acquire binding force it must be "generally acceptable." This condition may be regrettable, but those who wish to disregard it will have either to change the state system or trust that through such extralegal methods as diplomatic pressure the dissenting Members will be brought to acquiesce. Bowing to such pressure does not, however, necessarily signify a change in the Member's legal position . . . The Charter, however, probably reflects the maximum rather than the minimum of consensus that could have been reached at San Francisco.[17]

We applaud the author's honesty and refusal to bow to discouragement while we commiserate with his distress. But his analysis does little to show the way out of our own difficulties. Shall we throw up our hands? I hope not. We can try to regroup our wits and dig deeper into the Charter, the evidence, and the record.

The struggle within the United Nations over the status of non-self-governing peoples found its earliest focus in the territory of South West Africa. In the first meeting of the General Assembly in 1946, a debate concerning the territory

17 Leo Gross, "The United Nations and the Role of Law," 19 *International Organization* 538-539 (1965).

presaged the storms to come. The controversy over the territory has been the longest sustained of the many in the United Nations affecting non-self-governing peoples. It is also the dispute within which the most carefully planned and tenacious efforts have been made to define and settle the issues in legal terms through adjudication. If we would dig deeper, we will do well to dig here.

CHAPTER FOUR

SOUTH WEST AFRICA

IN THE INTERNATIONAL

COURT OF JUSTICE

World War I was carried into South West Africa, then a German colony, by troops of the Union of South Africa. By November 15, 1915, South African military control had substantially replaced the former German regime, and the South African Minister of Defense had proclaimed a South African Protectorate over the territory. When the war ended, the protectorate was converted into a mandate under Article 22 of the Covenant of the League of Nations. It was a mandate of the third class, called Class C, covering territories "which, owing to the sparseness of their population, or their small size, or their remoteness from the centers of civilization, or their geographical contiguity to the territory of the Mandatory . . . can be best administered under the laws of the Mandatory as integral portions of its territory, subject to the safeguards [stipulated in Article 22] in the interests of the indigenous population." On May 9, 1919, the British Crown accepted the mandate in behalf of the Government of the Union of South Africa (which confirmed the acceptance) and undertook to exercise it "on behalf of the League of Nations" in accordance with its provisions.

The Council of the League of Nations confirmed the mandate on December 17, 1920, and proclaimed its terms in a formal document containing a preamble and seven articles.[1]

Article 2 in a first paragraph vested in the Union of South Africa as the Mandatory "full power of administration and legislation over the territory . . . as an integral portion of the Union of South Africa." The second paragraph of Article 2, echoing Article 22 of the Covenant of the League of Nations, stipulated that the Mandatory "shall promote to the utmost the material and moral well-being and the social progress of the inhabitants of the territory." Articles 3, 4, and 5 contained a variety of explicit prohibitions and requirements concerning the slave trade, the sale of intoxicating liquor, traffic in arms and ammunition, military training of the natives, a guaranty of freedom of conscience and of the free exercise of all forms of worship, and the rights of missionaries from any member state of the League of Nations to pursue their calling. Article 6 required that the Mandatory "shall make to the Council of the League of Nations an annual report to the satisfaction of the Council, containing full information with regard to the territory, and indicating the measures taken to carry out the obligations assumed under Articles 2, 3, 4 and 5." Apart from the affirmation of the rights of missionaries, the terms of Articles 2 to 6 are customarily described as the "conduct provisions" of the mandate. Article 7 in its first paragraph required the "consent of the Council of the League of Nations . . . for any modifications

---

[1] League of Nations Doc. 21/31/14D (Dec. 17, 1920); *International Legislation*, ed. Manlay O. Hudson (Washington, D.C.: Carnegie Endowment for International Peace, 1931), I, 57.

of the terms" of the mandate. The second paragraph of Article 7 was to become a bone of contention in the International Court of Justice in litigation that traced a checkered course from 1960 to 1966. By its terms, the Mandatory "agrees that, if any dispute whatever should arise between the Mandatory and another member of the League of Nations relating to the interpretation or the application of the provisions of the Mandate, such dispute, if it cannot be settled by negotiation, shall be submitted to the Permanent Court of International Justice provided for by Article 14 of the Covenant of the League of Nations."

A tug of war set in early between the Union of South Africa and the Permanent Mandates Commission, constituted by the Council of the League of Nations as its instrument for overseeing the administration of the various territories under mandate. When the Union of South Africa and Portugal drew up an agreement to fix a boundary between South West Africa and Angola, the Union inserted into the preamble an assertion of its "full sovereignty over the territory of South-West Africa, lately under the sovereignty of Germany." On March 11, 1927, the Union's Prime Minister declared in Parliament that "sovereignty over South West Africa resides neither in the Principal Allied and Associated Powers, nor in the League of Nations, nor in the British Empire, but in the Government of the Union of South Africa." The Permanent Mandates Commission promptly nailed both statements. In a report to the Council of the League of Nations, the Commission expressed its anxiety "to know the exact meaning which is to be attributed to the expressions referred to" and hoped that the Government of the Union would "be so good as to explain" just what it meant.[2] The Union of South Africa, like Uncle Remus' tar baby, just said nothing.

The pulling and hauling continued. On March 2, 1936, the Union of South Africa, through its own so-called "Constitution Commission" for South West Africa, announced:

(a) The present form of government of the Territory [of South West Africa] is a failure and should be abolished.

(b) There is no legal obstacle to the government of the mandated territory as a province of the Union subject to the Mandate.[3]

In the same year, 1936, the Union of South Africa strode up to the brink, where it stayed poised. Insisting in its annual report to the Council of the League that no legal obstacle impeded the incorporation of the Territory in the Union as a fifth province, it went on to acknowledge that "sufficient grounds have not been adduced for taking such a step."[4] At intervals thereafter, South Africa reiterated its claims, and the Permanent Mandates Commission regularly countered the successive assertions. The issue continued to burn slowly, until the Second World War suspended the activities of the Permanent Mandates Commission.

When the League of Nations assembled in its terminal meetings at the end of World War II to dissolve in favor of

[2] Permanent Mandates Commission, Minutes, 11th Session (Annex 6), 204-205 (1927).

[3] Report of the South West Africa Commission (Pretoria, 1936), p. 77.

[4] Report of the Government of the Union of South Africa to the Council of the League Concerning the Administration of South West Africa for the Year 1936 (Pretoria, 1937), p. 4.

the United Nations, it sought to arrange an orderly transition for the various mandates to the new regime. The mandate over South West Africa stood out as a problem apart. The Union of South Africa persisted in its declared will to annex South West Africa. At the same time, the Union acknowledged its continuing responsibilities under the mandate, pledging that it "will continue to administer the Territory scrupulously in accordance with the obligations of the Mandate, for the advancement and promotion of the interests of the inhabitants." Acknowledging a prospect of technical difficulties in "compliance with the letter of the Mandate" because of the "disappearance of those organs of the League concerned with the supervision of mandates, primarily the Mandates Commission and the League Council," it reaffirmed its determination to comply in spirit: "The Union Government will nevertheless regard the dissolution of the League as in no way diminishing its obligations under the Mandate, which it will continue to discharge with the full and proper appreciation of its responsibilities until such time as other arrangements are agreed upon concerning the future status of the territory."[5]

The Assembly of the League responded by ignoring the threat and underscoring the obligation. In its final resolution concerning mandates, for which the Union of South Africa joined in voting, the Assembly explicitly recalled the governing principles of Article 22 of the Covenant. It went on to recognize that Chapters XI, XII, and XIII of the Charter of the United Nations embodied principles corre-

5 *League of Nations Official Journal,* Spec. Supp. 194, 21st Ass. (plenary, 1946), pp. 32-33.

sponding to those of Article 22 of the Covenant. Finally, it took "note of the expressed intentions of the Members of the League now administering territories under mandate to continue to administer them for the well-being and development of the peoples concerned in accordance with the obligations contained in the respective Mandates, until other arrangements have been agreed between the United Nations and the respective mandatory Powers."[6]

All territories other than South West Africa that had been under Class C mandates have long since been converted into trust territories by agreements between the original mandatory powers or their successors and the United Nations. South Africa alone has hewn to its isolated course.

In the very first General Assembly of the United Nations, the Union reaffirmed its desire to incorporate South West Africa and placed a plan for incorporation before the General Assembly. The General Assembly declined to accede to the proposal, recommending instead that the mandate be replaced by a United Nations trusteeship. The Union in its turn rejected the General Assembly's recommendation, but softened its refusal by reaffirming its earlier declaration that it would continue to honor its obligations under the mandate. So the old tug of war between the Union of South Africa and the Permanent Mandates Commission of the League of Nations was revived in the United Nations.

In 1948, the Trusteeship Council of the United Nations broke through the formal surface of interchanges between South Africa and the United Nations to dig into the facts

6 *Ibid.*, p. 58.

below. Analyzing the budget submitted by South Africa for South West Africa, the Council observed that only 10 percent of it had been expended on "the indigenous inhabitants, who comprise approximately 90 percent of the entire population." The Council considered "that great efforts should be made to eliminate, through education and other positive measures, whatever reasons may exist that explain segregation." Distressed to observe "that no educational facilities are provided by the Government in the purely indigenous areas," the Trusteeship Council stressed that the "provision of urgently-needed educational facilities for the indigenous population is vital to their political, economic and social development."[7]

The opposing positions hardened through 1948 and 1949. In November 1948, South Africa's representative in the Fourth Committee blandly referred to "the previous Mandate, since expired."[8] In July 1949, South Africa let it be known that it would no longer submit reports on South West Africa to the United Nations. In its view, "the submission of information has provided an opportunity to utilize the Trusteeship Council . . . as a forum for unjustified criticism and censure of the Union Government's administration, not only in South-West Africa but in the Union as well . . . the very act of submitting a report has created in the minds of a number of Members of the United Nations an impression that the Trusteeship Council is competent to make recommendations on matters of internal administra-

---

7 U.N. Gen. Ass. Off. Rec. 3rd Sess., Supp. No. 4, pp. 42-45 (A/603) (1948).
8 U.N. Ass. Off. Rec. 3rd Sess., 1st Part, 4th Comm., p. 293 (1948).

tion of South West Africa and has fostered other misconceptions regarding the status of this Territory."[9]

The General Assembly responded to South African defiance by asserting the claims of law. It submitted a general question and three particular questions to the International Court of Justice for an advisory opinion. In general, the Assembly wanted to know: "what is the international status of the Territory of South West Africa and what are the international obligations of the Union of South Africa arising therefrom?" In particular, it asked:

> (a) Does the Union of South Africa continue to have international obligations under the Mandate for South West Africa and, if so, what are those obligations?
> (b) Are the provisions of Chapter XII of the Charter applicable and, if so, in what manner, to the Territory of South West Africa?
> (c) Has the Union of South Africa the competence to modify the international status of the Territory of South West Africa or, in the event of a negative reply, where does competence rest to determine and modify the international status of the Territory?

Pursuant to the statute and rules of the Court, notice was given to all states entitled to appear. All members of the United Nations were informed that the Court would receive any written statements from them on the questions that they might care to submit. Written statements were filed by the Union of South Africa, Egypt, India, Poland, and the

9 U.N. Gen. Ass. Off. Rec. 4th Sess., 4th Comm., Annex to Summary Records of Meetings, p. 7 (U.N. Doc. A/929) (1949).

United States. Oral presentations were made by the Union of South Africa, the Philippines, and the Secretary General of the United Nations.

The Court was unanimous on the general question. It advised the General Assembly that South West Africa "is a territory under the International Mandate assumed by the Union of South Africa on December 17, 1920." On question (a), the Court was nearly unanimous. By a vote of twelve judges to two, it advised the General Assembly "that the Union of South Africa continues to have the international obligations stated in Article 22 of the Covenant of the League of Nations and in the Mandate for South West Africa as well as the obligation to transmit petitions from the inhabitants of that Territory, the supervisory functions [theretofore exercised by the League of Nations] to be exercised by the United Nations, to which the annual reports and the petitions are to be submitted, and the reference to the Permanent Court of International Justice to be replaced by a reference to the International Court of Justice, in accordance with Article 7 of the Mandate and Article 37 of the Statutes of the Court." The Court returned to unanimity on the first part of question (b), advising the General Assembly "that the provisions of Chapter XII of the Charter are applicable to the Territory of South West Africa in the sense that they provide a means by which the Territory may be brought under the Trusteeship System." The Court divided sharply, however, on the second part of question (b). By a vote of eight judges to six, it concluded "that the provisions of Chapter XII of the Charter do not impose on the Union of South Africa a legal obligation to place the Territory under the Trusteeship System." Finally, on question (c), the Court, again unanimous, advised "that the Union of South Africa acting alone has not the competence to modify the international status of the Territory of South West Africa, and that the competence to determine and modify the international status of the Territory rests with the Union of South Africa acting with the consent of the United Nations."[10]

In 1950, the General Assembly accepted the Advisory Opinion,[11] and created an *Ad Hoc* Committee to confer with the Union of South Africa concerning procedural measures to implement the Opinion. But South Africa remained obdurate. In meeting after meeting of its representatives with the *Ad Hoc* Committee, South Africa reargued the contentions that it had submitted to the International Court of Justice. Rejecting both the Advisory Opinion and the endorsement of the Opinion by the General Assembly, it continued to insist that the mandate had lapsed and that South Africa was no longer bound by its terms.

In 1952, the General Assembly reminded South Africa that it "cannot avoid its international obligations by unilateral action" and that the "United Nations cannot recognize as valid any measures taken unilaterally by the Union of South Africa which would modify the international status of the Territory of South West Africa."[12] Again in 1953, the Gen-

10 International Status of South West Africa, Advisory Opinion of July 11, 1950, ICJ Rep. 1950, pp. 128, 143-144.

11 Gen. Ass. Res. 449A (V) (Dec. 13, 1950), U.N. Gen. Ass. Off. Rec. 5th Sess., Supp. No. 20, pp. 55-56 (A/1775).

12 Gen. Ass. Res. 570 (VI) (Jan. 19, 1952), U.N. Gen. Ass. Off. Rec. 6th Sess., Supp. No. 20, pp. 63-64 (A/2119).

eral Assembly deeply regretted "that the Government of the Union of South Africa continues in its refusal to assist in the implementation of the advisory opinion of the International Court of Justice concerning South West Africa" It appealed solemnly to South Africa "to reconsider its position," with a warning "that the Territory of South West Africa is a Territory under the international Mandate assumed by the Union of South Africa on 17 December 1920."[13]

So the dreary experience dragged on. In 1955, the Union challenged the voting procedure within the General Assembly, contrasting it with the voting system under the League of Nations in which questions regarding mandates had to be decided by unanimous votes. Still relying on law to curb South African intransigence, the General Assembly again turned to the International Court of Justice for an advisory opinion. On this occasion, South Africa neither submitted a written statement nor requested to be heard. The Court in a unanimous opinion advised the General Assembly that decisions of questions relating to reports and petitions concerning the Territory of South West Africa should be regarded as important questions within the meaning of Article 18, Paragraph 2, of the Charter of the United Nations, requiring disposition by a two-thirds vote.[14] South Africa remained unimpressed. Its Minister for External Affairs did "not care tuppence whether the United Nations observes

13 Gen. Ass. Res. 749A (VIII), (Nov. 28, 1953), U.N. Gen. Ass. Off. Rec. 8th Sess., Supp. No. 17, pp. 26-27 (A/2630).
14 Voting Procedure on Questions Relating to Reports and Petitions Concerning the Territory of South West Africa, Advisory Opinion, ICJ Rep. 1955, pp. 67, 78 (June 7, 1955).

the two-thirds majority rule or the unanimity rule in dealing with South West African affairs because we have consistently said the United Nations has no right to concern
itself with the affairs of South West Africa."[15]

Toward the end of 1955, the General Assembly's Committee on South West Africa proposed to conduct oral hearings at which representatives of the population of the
Territory might appear. Before undertaking such hearings,
the General Assembly again sought the advice of the International Court of Justice. South Africa again held itself
aloof from the proceedings. In examining the problem, the
Court reaffirmed its earlier statement that "the effective performance of the sacred trust of civilization by the Mandatory
Powers required that the administration of the mandated
territories should be subject to international supervision"
and that the "necessity for supervision continues . . . despite
the disappearance [of the League of Nations]." It also reiterated that "the General Assembly [of the United Nations]
had replaced the Council of the League as the supervisory
organ." On the precise question submitted, it advised the
General Assembly that oral hearings could properly be
granted to petitioners by the General Assembly through its
Committee on South West Africa.[16]

The succession of advisory opinions did not dissipate the
general frustration. In 1957, the General Assembly tried
another tack. It established a Good Offices Committee, con-

<hr>

15 235 South Africa 511, June 25, 1955, cited in Memorial submitted by the
Government of Ethiopia, p. 38.

16 Admissibility of Hearings of Petitioners by the Committee on South
West Africa, Advisory Opinion, ICJ Rep. 1956, pp. 23, 27, 29, 32 (June 1,
1956). The Court reached its opinion by eight votes to five.

sisting of representatives of the United States, the United Kingdom, and Brazil, to explore a possible basis for an agreement with South Africa that might effectively maintain the international status of South West Africa. Meanwhile, the Committee on South West Africa persevered in its fruitless labors.

It came as no surprise when the Good Offices Committee, after two years of effort, reported in 1959 that it could find no basis for an understanding with the Mandatory Power. The Committee on South West Africa on its part submitted a report on conditions in the Territory that recited a tale of unrelieved gloom. Ignoring the obligation "to promote to the utmost the material and moral well-being and the social progress of the inhabitants," the Union of South Africa as mandatory had continued to exclude the indigenous population from any realistic participation in "the political, economic, social and educational life of the Territory." The native majority had been "subjected to unnatural restrictions on their freedom of movement and regulation of their daily life," their interests had been disregarded, and the denial of present opportunity and hope for the future had been crystallized into a systematic application of apartheid.[17]

South Africa dug its heels in deeper, and the African and Asian states fumed. In June 1960, the Second Conference of Independent African States convened at Addis Ababa. Their mood was to force the issue. Exploring strategy and tactics, they decided to move along two mutually supporting lines. They would mount a renewed and strenuous effort in the

[17] Report of the Committee on South West Africa, U.N. Gen. Ass. Off. Rec. 14th Sess., Supp. No. 12, pp. 32-33 (A/4191) (1959).

General Assembly, and bring a contentious proceeding in the International Court of Justice. The governments of Ethiopia and Liberia, which had been members of the League of Nations, undertook to institute the proceeding.

The Fifteenth General Assembly supported the decision of Ethiopia and Liberia to litigate by adopting Resolution No. 1565.[18] In the resolution, the General Assembly recited the long record of futility that had attended the efforts of the *Ad Hoc* Committee, the Committee on South West Africa, and the Good Offices Committee; proclaimed that the mandatory had "failed and refused to carry out its obligations under the Mandate"; concluded that a dispute had arisen between Ethiopia, Liberia, and other member states on the one hand and the Union of South Africa on the other which could not be settled by negotiation; and commended Ethiopia and Liberia for their initiative in submitting the dispute to the International Court of Justice pursuant to Article 7 of the mandate.

Ethiopia and Liberia filed their applications in the International Court of Justice on November 4, 1960. In their applications they requested the Court to adjudge that:

1. South West Africa remained a Territory under the mandate.

2. The Union of South Africa as the mandatory power remained subject to the obligations of the mandate and of Article 22 of the Covenant of the League; the General Assembly of the United Nations had succeeded to the supervisory responsibilities of the League of Nations; and the Union was under an obligation to submit to such super-

18 U.N. Gen. Ass. Off. Rec. 15th Sess., Supp. No. 16, pp. 31-32 (A/4684) (1960).

vision by the General Assembly in regard to the exercise of the mandate.

3. South Africa was bound to transmit petitions from the inhabitants of South West Africa to the United Nations, and to submit an annual report satisfactory to the United Nations.

4. South Africa had modified the terms of the mandate substantially without the consent of the United Nations, in violation of the mandate and Article 22 of the Covenant.

5. South Africa had violated Article 2 of the mandate and Article 22 of the Covenant by failing to promote the material and moral well-being and social progress of the inhabitants of the territory, in violation of its duty under the mandate.

6. South Africa had practiced apartheid in violation of Article 2 of the mandate and Article 22 of the Covenant; and it must forthwith cease to do so.

7. South Africa had violated the mandate by adopting legislation, regulations, proclamations, and administrative decrees that were arbitrary, unreasonable, unjust, and detrimental to human dignity, and must immediately repeal such measures.

8. South Africa had suppressed the rights and liberties of the inhabitants of the Territory essential to their orderly evolution toward self-government, in violation of the mandate and the Covenant of the League.

9. South Africa had exercised powers of administration and legislation over the Territory that were inconsistent with the international status of the Territory, in violation of the terms of the mandate and Article 22 of the Covenant.

10. South Africa had violated Article 6 of the mandate

by failing to render annual reports to the General Assembly.

11. South Africa had failed to transmit petitions from the inhabitants of the Territory, in violation of the mandate and the Covenant of the League.

In their supporting Memorials, Ethiopia and Liberia re-newed and amplified the foregoing allegations and requests and added another concerning military bases. In the submissions (roughly equivalent to a request for findings and a prayer for relief in American legal practice), they asked the Court to find that South Africa had violated Article 4 of the mandate and Article 22 of the Covenant by establishing military bases within the Territory.

On November 30, 1961, a little more than a year after the filing of the applications, South Africa filed four preliminary objections, praying the Court to decide that the governments of Ethiopia and Liberia had no *locus standi* and that the Court itself lacked jurisdiction to adjudicate upon the questions of fact and law raised in the Applications and Memorials of the applicants. In accordance with its rules (Article 62, paragraph 3), the Court suspended the proceedings on the merits and set the cases down for hearing on the preliminary objections, to begin on March 1, 1962.

In its first preliminary objection, South Africa asserted that the Mandate for South West Africa had never been and was no longer a treaty or convention in force within the meaning of Article 37 of the Statute of the International Court of Justice. In the second preliminary objection, South Africa contended that the applicants' governments were neither of them "another member of the League of Nations" as required for *locus standi* under Article 7 of the mandate.

In the third objection, South Africa insisted that the disagreement between the applicants and itself was not a "dispute" as envisaged in Article 7 of the mandate, "more particularly in that no material interests of the Governments of Ethiopia and/or Liberia or of their nationals are involved therein or affected thereby." In the fourth preliminary objection, South Africa protested that the alleged dispute was not one which "cannot be settled by negotiation" within the meaning of Article 7 of the mandate.[19]

On December 21, 1962, the Court handed down its judgment, by an eight to seven vote. It found that it had jurisdiction to adjudicate upon the merits of the dispute.

In quashing the first objection, the Court explicitly reaffirmed the position taken in the Advisory Opinion of July 11, 1950. The mandate was "a special type of instrument composite in nature and instituting a novel international regime."[20] Although it took the form of a resolution of the Council of the League of Nations, it could not be "correctly regarded as embodying only an executive action in pursuance of the Covenant. The Mandate, in fact and in law, is an international agreement having the character of a treaty or convention."[21] Despite the dissolution of the League of Nations, the mandate remained in effect:

The unanimous holding of the Court in 1950 on the survival and continuing effect of Article 7 of the Man-

[19] The terms of the several objections are here quoted from the submissions presented by South Africa at the hearing on October 11, 1962. See South West Africa Cases, Preliminary Objections, ICJ Rep. 1962, pp. 326-327.
[20] South West Africa Cases, Preliminary Objections, ICJ Rep. 1962, pp. 319, 331 (Dec. 21, 1962).
[21] *Ibid.*, p. 330.

date, continues to reflect the Court's opinion today. Nothing has since occurred which would warrant the Court reconsidering it. All important facts were stated or referred to in the proceedings before the Court in 1950.

The Court finds that though the League of Nations and the Permanent Court of International Justice have both ceased to exist, the obligation of the Respondent to submit to the compulsory jurisdiction of that Court was effectively transferred to this Court before the dissolution of the League of Nations . . .

This transferred obligation was voluntarily assumed by the Respondent when joining the United Nations. There could be no question of lack of consent on the part of the Respondent as regards this transfer to this Court of the Respondent's obligation under Article 7 of the Mandate to submit to the compulsory jurisdiction of the Permanent Court. The validity of Article 7, in the Court's view, was not affected by the dissolution of the League, just as the Mandate as a whole is still in force for the reasons stated above.[22]

To ram the point home, the Court reminded South Africa of the source of its alleged authority. The sole authority that South Africa had over the Territory of South West Africa was based on the mandate. "If the Mandate lapsed, as the Union Government contends, the latter's authority would equally have lapsed. To retain the rights derived from the

22 *Ibid.*, pp. 334-335.

Mandate and to deny the obligations thereunder could not be justified."[23]

Turning to South Africa's second preliminary objection, the Court analyzed the events attending the dissolution of the League of Nations and the final resolution adopted by the League before its demise. From the analysis, the Court concluded that Ethiopia and Liberia retained the status of "another Member of the League of Nations" within the meaning of Article 7 of the mandate. South Africa's second preliminary objection that neither applicant was "another member of the League of Nations," as required for *locus standi*,[24] was accordingly rejected.

I pass over the third preliminary objection for the moment. In dismissing the fourth, the Court found that the recurrent frustration of attempts at adjustment in the League of Nations and the United Nations over the years sufficiently demonstrated that the dispute between the applicant states and South Africa could not be settled by negotiation.

It is the Court's disposition of the third preliminary objection that especially requires our attention, if we are to have any hope of understanding the bewildering discrepancy between the first judgment of the International Court of Justice in the South West Africa Cases and the second. I remind you of the terms of the third preliminary objection: "the conflict or disagreement alleged by the Governments of Ethiopia and Liberia to exist between them and the Govern-

23 *Ibid.*, p. 333, quoting from International Status of South West Africa, Advisory Opinion of July 11, 1950, ICJ Rep. 1950, p. 133.

24 *Ibid.*, pp. 327, 342.

ment of the Republic of South Africa, is by reason of its nature and content not a 'dispute' as envisaged in Article 7 of the Mandate for South West Africa, more particularly in that no material interests of the Governments of Ethiopia and /or Liberia or of their nationals are involved therein or affected thereby."[25] In support, South Africa argued that courts of law "are not concerned with conflicts, differences of opinion or opposite views unconnected with the rights or legal interests of the litigants. It is submitted that the position is the same in International Law. International Courts exist for the adjudication and settlement of claims arising from legal rights or legal interests and are not there for judicial expression on differences of opinion or on conflicts of views between States, unrelated to their legal rights or interests."[26]

In sum, South Africa contended that whatever disputes there might be between the applicants and itself, they were not disputes in any justiciable sense. In its view, only a dispute arising out of an alleged injury by South Africa to a specific material interest of Ethiopia or Liberia or of one of their nationals would be justiciable; and neither applicant had alleged any such injury. For example, although under Article 5 of the mandate, South Africa had bound itself to "allow all missionaries, nationals of any State Member of the League of Nations, to enter into, travel and reside in the Territory for the purpose of prosecuting their calling," neither applicant had charged that any of its nationals had

25 *Ibid.*, p. 327. *Cf.* Preliminary Objections Filed by the Government of the Republic of South Africa, November 1961, p. 1.
26 Preliminary Objections Filed by the Government of the Republic of South Africa, November 1961, p. 164.

been denied the right to enter in a missionary capacity. Neither applicant had alleged any denial by South Africa to any national of the applicant of an opportunity to enter the Territory nor to pass through it nor to trade within it, whatever rights of entry, transit or trade there may have been under the mandate. In effect, South Africa insisted, Ethiopia and Liberia were bringing representative suits in behalf of all the African states, in an effort to transfer to the International Court of Justice the very issues under the conduct provisions of the mandate that had been argued recurrently in the League of Nations and in the General Assembly of the United Nations.

It may be helpful to pause for a moment to invoke an analogy to a charitable trustee in Anglo-American law, provided we do so with an abundance of caution. There are many rocks on which attempts to draw analogies between institutions in different legal systems can founder. The appearance of analogy can lie in the eye of the observer, which unconsciously sorts out data that seem to fit a familiar pattern from an unfamiliar context in which real differences lie undetected. But the comparative method can be richly rewarding if pursued with insight, care and restraint. Let us risk it here.

Who may enforce a charitable trust of, let us say, a large tract of beautiful land with historic associations donated for public enjoyment by a former owner? It is hornbook law that the Attorney General represents the community in seeing to it that such a trust is carried out in accordance with its terms. A member of the public has no standing to institute a proceeding to enforce such a trust unless he can demonstrate that he has a "special interest." Cases are legion on what is required to establish such a "special interest." In broad terms, a member of the public will be found to have such a special interest only if he is entitled to receive a benefit under the trust that is something more than the benefit accruing to members of the public in general. Professor Austin Scott illuminates the question through representative cases. Where a testator left his estate in trust to establish and maintain an art museum in a city, a tax-paying resident was denied standing to sue to enforce the trust.[27] Where an estate was left in trust to maintain a home for needy female teachers in a county in Connecticut, the practical interest of a group of needy teachers in the execution of the trust was held insufficient to qualify them as parties to institute a proceeding to enforce it.[28] But there are other cases with other results. For example, in a number of cases where a trust was established for the benefit of the poor of a particular church or parish or town, churchwardens or church members of the particular church or inhabitants of the particular parish or town were permitted to bring suits (in behalf of themselves and others similarly situated) to enforce the trust.[29] Our own law thus recognizes occasions when the interest of a responsible member of the community in the general purposes of a charitable trust is deemed to constitute a sufficient "special interest" to support enforcement proceedings by him. In such cases, Anglo-American legal doctrine permits alternative procedures for enforcement, either by such members of

27 4 Scott on Trusts (2nd ed.), § 391 (p. 2762), citing Dickey v. Volker, 321 Mo. 235, 11 S.W. 2d 278 (1928).
28 *Ibid.*, citing Averill v. Lewis, 106 Conn. 582, 138 Atl. 815 (1927).
29 *Ibid.*, p. 2759.

the community or by the Attorney General (or another public official designated by statute).

I turn back to the South West Africa Cases. If we were to rephrase South Africa's third preliminary objection in the language of charitable trusts, South Africa contended in effect that Ethiopia and Liberia were merely members of the general international public seeking to assert the general interest but lacking a sufficient special interest of their own to warrant the proceeding. In support of its contention, South Africa cited the applicants' own words to confound them. In their Memorials, the applicants had asserted they had "a legal interest in seeing to it through judicial process that the sacred trust of civilization created by the Mandate is not violated."[30] If South Africa's view of the matter were accepted, with whom would responsibility lie for carrying out the "sacred trust"? Who could exercise a responsibility comparable to that vested under English and American law in the Attorney General or some statutorily designated public officer or body?

One's mind turns naturally to the General Assembly of the United Nations. The General Assembly had been pronounced the successor to the earlier responsibilities of the Council of the League of Nations under the mandate, in the International Court of Justice's Advisory Opinion of July 11, 1950. In rejecting the first two preliminary objections of the Respondent in the litigated South West Africa Cases of 1962, the Court had reaffirmed the conclusions of the Advisory Opinion. But if we should try to push our analogy to the point of contemplating a proceeding by the

30 Memorial Submitted by the Government of Ethiopia, April 1961, pp. 62-63.

United Nations itself in the International Court of Justice
to enforce the "sacred trust," we would strike a rock in
Article 34 of the Statute of the Court. Under Article 34,
"Only states may be parties in cases before the Court." The
United Nations itself may not. If none but the United Nations had standing to institute a proceeding in the International Court of Justice under Article 7 of the mandate, such
a proceeding could be instituted by no one at all. The judicial supervision contemplated by Article 7 of the mandate
would disappear.

The International Court of Justice in the South West
Africa Cases declined to permit the disappearance of judicial supervision. In its view, Article 6 and Article 7 of the
mandate provided parallel and mutually supporting procedures for enforcement. Article 6 vested responsibility for
administrative supervision in the Council of the League of
Nations. Article 7 provided for "judicial protection by the
Permanent Court by vesting the right of invoking the compulsory jurisdiction against the Mandatory for the same
purpose in each of the other Members of the League."[31]
Although Article 7 of course contemplated protection of the
material interests of the Members or their nationals, it was
by no means confined to such protection. The "well-being
and development of the inhabitants of the Mandated territory [were] not less important."[32] Each Member of the
League had "a legal right or interest in the observance by
the Mandatory of its obligations . . . toward the inhabitants
of the Mandated Territory."[33]

[31] South West Africa Cases, Preliminary Objections, ICJ Rep. 1962, pp. 319,
344.
[32] *Ibid.*
[33] *Ibid.*, p. 343.

In a concurring opinion, Judge Jessup endorsed the conclusion and found support for it not only in the terms of the mandate but also in the nature of judicial responsibility under international law. "International law," he stressed, "has long recognized that States may have legal interests in matters which do not affect their financial, economic, or other 'material,' or, say, 'physical' or 'tangible' interests. One type of illustration of this principle of international law is to be found in the right of a State to concern itself, on general humanitarian grounds, with atrocities affecting human beings in another country . . . States have also asserted a legal interest in the general observance of the rules of international law."[34]

Among the seven dissenting opinions, I take the joint opinion filed by Judges Spender and Fitzmaurice as the most revealing. They would have upheld the third preliminary objection. In their view, the *travaux préparatoires* (legislative history) made it clear that the only disputes contemplated by Article 7 of the mandate were disputes arising out of an alleged infraction of some tangible or material right of a State. They endorsed the contention of South Africa that Liberia and Ethiopia were in effect appearing in a representational capacity, seeking to raise again in the International Court of Justice all the questions that had been agitated in political terms over the years in the United Nations General Assembly.

The particular arguments of Judges Spender and Fitzmaurice are illuminated by their general posture, exhibited in the opening paragraphs of their joint opinion. They re-

[34] South West Africa Cases, Preliminary Objections, ICJ Rep. 1962, pp. 319, 425.

proached the majority for permitting their analysis of the
particular issues to have been swayed by a predisposition,
"namely that it is desirable and right that a provision for the
compulsory adjudication of certain disputes, which figures
(or did figure) as part of an institution—the Mandate for
South-West Africa—which is still in existence as an institution, should not be held to have become inoperative merely
on account of a change of circumstances—provided that this
change has not affected the *physical* possibility of continued
performance" (italics in the original).[35] They were not "un-
mindful of, nor . . . insensible to, the various considerations
of a non-juridical character, social, humanitarian and other,
which underlie this case."[36] But these were matters for political rather than legal determinations:

> It is apparent from the Memorials in the present
> case, that what the Court will principally be asked to
> decide on the merits is whether, in a number of dif-
> ferent respects, the Respondent State, as Mandatory, is
> in breach of its obligation under Article 2 of the Man-
> date to "promote to its utmost the material and moral
> well-being and the social progress of the inhabitants of
> the territory" . . . There is hardly a word in this sen-
> tence which has not now become loaded with a variety
> of overtones and associations. There is hardly a term
> which would not require prior objective definition, or
> redefinition, before it could justifiably be applied to the
> determination of a concrete legal issue. There is hardly

35 *Ibid.*, pp. 319, 465.
36 *Ibid.*, p. 466.

a term which could not be applied in widely different ways to the same situation or set of facts, according to differing subjective views as to what it meant, or ought to mean in the context; and it is a foregone conclusion that, in the absence of objective criteria, a large element of subjectivity must enter into any attempt to apply these terms to the facts of a given case. They involve questions of appreciation rather than of objective determination. As at present advised we have serious misgivings as to the legal basis on which the necessary objective criteria can be founded.

The proper forum for the appreciation and application of a provision of this kind is unquestionably a technical or political one, such as (formerly) the Permanent Mandates Commission, or the Council of the League of Nations—or today (as regards Trusteeships), the Trusteeship Council and the Assembly of the United Nations. But the fact that, in present circumstances, such technical or political control cannot in practice be exercised in respect of the Mandate for South-West Africa, is not a ground for asking a Court of law to discharge a task which, in the final analysis, hardly appears to be a judicial one.

The above considerations, in our opinion, strongly reinforce the view which, on other grounds, we have taken as to the third preliminary objection, namely that disputes about the conduct of the Mandate in relation to the "sacred trust" (as opposed to disputes about the individual statal interests of the Members of the League under the terms of the Mandate) are not the kind of disputes to which the compulsory adjudication clause of the Mandate was intended to, or did, apply.[37]

The language of Judges Spender and Fitzmaurice will ring familiarly in the ears of American lawyers. In the terms of American constitutional law, they would have declined jurisdiction on the ground that the questions raised on the merits were "political questions." Looking beyond the jurisdictional question raised under Article 7 of the mandate, they were stirred to apprehension by the applicants' requests under Article 2. It is Article 2 that obligated South Africa as the mandatory power to "promote to the utmost the material and moral well-being and social progress of the inhabitants of the territory." Dismayed by the prospect of applying the criteria of Article 2, Judges Spender and Fitzmaurice regarded the "subjective" and "political" nature of those criteria as supporting reasons for a restrictive interpretation of Article 7.

Judge Jessup was not dismayed. Unlike the judgment of the majority, he met the dissenting brethren explicitly and head on.[38] As an American lawyer, he derived his concept of the proper scope of judicial action not only from the practice of common law judges but also from constitutional adjudication by the Supreme Court of the United States. "Certainly," he reminded his colleagues, "courts can deter-

---

37 *Ibid.*, pp. 466-467.

38 The majority judgment must be taken to have rejected the contentions of Judges Spender and Fitzmaurice. It must be assumed that the Spender-Fitzmaurice views had been expressed in the deliberations in chambers preceding the issuance of the judgment, and the majority decided that the applicants had a legal right or interest within the meaning of Article 7 of the mandate. But the majority judgment did not expressly examine the particular arguments of Judges Spender and Fitzmaurice here discussed.

mine and have determined whether particular laws or actions comply with general broad criteria such as 'due process,' 'equal protection' and 'religious freedom.' The Supreme Court of the United States is able to determine what measures are or are not compatible with religious freedom (Reynolds v. United States (1879) 98 U.S. 244; Engel *et al* v. Vitale (1962) 370 U.S. 421); or what is 'the liberty in a social organization which requires the protection of law against the evils which menace the health, safety, morals and welfare of the people' (West Coast Hotel Co. v. Parrish (1937) 300 U.S. 379, 391)."[39]

We do not know how these arguments of Judge Jessup may have been received by Judge Spender of Australia, Judge Fitzmaurice of Britain, or the dissenting judges from civil law systems. Conceivably, they might have argued that international law was still too rudimentary as compared with a mature national legal system and that the International Court of Justice was too new and untried a tribunal as compared with the high courts of old and established national legal systems to warrant the International Court of Justice in taking on a burden of decision that might well be properly borne by the Supreme Court of the United States. If and to the extent that this were their concern, it might not have been ill-founded, provided that it were balanced by an awareness of the responsibility of the International Court of Justice to foster its own evolution in harmony with the purposes and principles of the Charter of the United Nations. Neither American constitutional doctrine nor the

[39] Separate opinion of Judge Jessup in South West Africa Cases: Preliminary Objections, ICJ Rep. 1962, pp. 319, 428,

Supreme Court of the United States burst full grown from
the brows of the Founding Fathers. The content of the
doctrine and the powers and duties of the court evolved
through successive tests and applications, in which neither
the direction nor the nature of the evolution was predeter-
mined. Especially in the early formative years, the course
of development depended on the key participants' appreciation of what was at stake and their feeling of responsibility
toward the future. In the first few weeks of his presidency,
George Washington stressed that "Many things which appear of little importance in themselves and at the beginning,
may have great and durable consequences from their having
been established at the commencement of a new general
government."[40] In a comparable outlook, Chief Justice
Marshall adjured his colleagues and countrymen: "we must
never forget that it is a constitution we are expounding . . .
a constitution intended to endure for ages to come, and,
consequently, to be adapted to the various crises of human
affairs."[41] As the justices of the Supreme Court must be
mindful of the place of the Court in the general scheme of
government of the United States, so the judges of the International Court of Justice should be alive to the functions
of the Court within the United Nations system. The International Court of Justice is more than the most important
among international judicial tribunals. It is established as
one of the six principal organs of the United Nations, along
with the General Assembly, Security Council, Economic and

---

[40] *The Writings of George Washington,* ed. John C. Fitzpatrick (George
Washington Bicentennial Edition; Washington, D.C.: GPO, 1939), XXX, 321.
[41] McCulloch v. Maryland, 4 Wheat. 316, 407, 415, 4 Law Ed. 579, 602,
603-604 (1819).

Social Council, Trusteeship Council, and Secretariat; and its statute forms an integral part of the Charter.

We come to the South West Africa Cases, Second Phase.[42] Following the dismissal of the four preliminary objections, dates were set by the International Court of Justice for the filing of "the further pleadings on the merits." The last of the pleadings, a rejoinder by the government of South Africa, was filed on December 23, 1964, and the cases became ready for hearing. Public sittings of the Court were held during the periods March 15 to July 14, 1965, and September 20 to November 29, 1965. During these public sittings, the Court received the testimony of a long array of witnesses and experts called by the government of South Africa. No witnesses were called by the applicants, who relied on depositions and written statements as the vehicles for evidence in support of their claims. The Court also heard extensive oral arguments. On July 18, 1966, the Court handed down its judgment. It found "that the Applicants cannot be considered to have established any legal right or interest appertaining to them in the subject-matter of the present claims, and that, accordingly, the Court must decline to give effect to them."[43]

The international legal community blinked increduously. On its face, the decision of 1966 appeared to speak in direct contradiction to the rejection of the third preliminary objection by the judgment of 1962. The Court in 1962 had decided that each applicant had "a legal right or interest

[42] The South West Africa Cases (Ethiopia v. South Africa; Liberia v. South Africa) Second Phase, ICJ Rep. 1966, p. 6 (July 18, 1966).
[43] Ibid., p. 51.

in the observance by the Mandatory of its obligations . . .
toward the inhabitants of the Mandated Territory."[44] Besides, what had happened to the issues on the merits that had
been the entire focus of consideration in the Second Phase?

In the opinion supporting the 1966 judgment, the Court
offered the following explanation:

> In the course of the proceedings on the merits, com-
> prising the exchange of written pleadings, the oral argu-
> ments of the Parties and the hearing of a considerable
> number of witnesses, the Parties put forward various
> contentions . . .
>
> On all these matters, the Court has studied the writ-
> ten pleadings and oral arguments of the Parties, and
> has also given consideration to the question of the order
> in which the various issues would fall to be dealt with.
> In this connection, there was one matter that apper-
> tained to the merits of the case but which had an ante-
> cedent character, namely the question of the Appli-
> cants' standing in the present phase of the proceedings,
> —not, that is to say, of their standing before the Court
> itself which was the subject of the Court's decision in
> 1962, but the question, as a matter of the merits of the
> case, of their legal right or interest regarding the sub-
> ject-matter of their claim, as set out in their final sub-
> missions.[45]

The Court appeared to be drawing a distinction between

44 South West Africa Cases, Preliminary Objections, ICJ Rep. 1962, pp. 319,
343.

45 South West Africa Cases, Second Phase, ICJ Rep. 1966, pp. 6, 17-18 (July
18, 1966).

the standing of a party to sue and his standing to receive a judgment on the merits in his lawsuit. Perhaps you find the explanation hard to follow. So do I. So did seven of the judges of the Court. As Judge Jessup put it:

This is the fifth time the Court has given consideration to legal matters arising out of the administration by the Republic of South Africa of the mandated territory of South West Africa. In the course of three Advisory Opinions rendered in 1950, 1955 and 1956, and in its Judgment of 21 December 1962, the Court never deviated from its conclusion that the Mandate survived the dissolution of the League of Nations and that South-West Africa is still a territory subject to the Mandate. By its judgment of today, the Court in effect decides that Applicants have no standing to ask the Court even for a declaration that the territory is still subject to the Mandate . . .

The Judgment of the Court rests upon the assertion that even though—as the Court decided in 1962—the Applicants had *locus standi* to institute the actions in this case, this does not mean that they have the legal interest which would entitle them to a judgment on the merits. No authority is produced in support of this assertion which suggests a procedure of utter futility. Why should any State institute any proceeding if it lacked standing to have judgment rendered in its favour if it succeeded in establishing its legal or factual contentions on the merits? Why would the Court tolerate a situation in which the parties would be put to great trouble and expense to explore all of the details of the merits, and only thereafter be told that the Court would pay no heed to all their arguments and evidence because the case was dismissed on a preliminary ground which precluded any investigation of the merits?[46]

The confusion generated by the decision was compounded by the division in the Court and a background of changes in its membership. In August 1965, just after an important part of the oral proceedings had been completed, Judge Badawi of the United Arab Republic died. He had joined with the majority in the judgment of 1962. Judge Busta-mante of Peru, also one of the majority in the 1962 judg-ment, had missed most of the oral proceedings because of illness and had therefore taken no part in the final judg-ment. Judge Zafrullah Khan of Pakistan did not participate. In consequence, of the fifteen judges of the Court, only twelve sat. They were joined by two judges *ad hoc,* Judge Mbanefo, named in behalf of the applicants, and Judge Van Wyk, appointed in behalf of the respondents. The four-teen judges divided evenly, seven to seven. Under the Stat-ute of the Court, "In the event of an equality of votes, the President . . . shall have a casting vote."[47] The casting vote in such a case supplements the initial vote entered by the President in his capacity as a judge of the Court. The tie was broken by the second—"casting"—vote of the President of the Court, Judge Spender.

---

[46] South West Africa Cases, Second Phase, ICJ Rep. 1966, pp. 6, 327, 382.
[47] Statute of the Court, Art. 55, para. 2.

CHAPTER FIVE

FROM THE COURT TO

THE GENERAL ASSEMBLY

I

I acknowledge my own perturbation at the procedural peculiarities of the two South West Africa cases. But it will not promote the larger purposes of our inquiry to dwell upon them. We would do well to bear in mind that the judgment on the preliminary objections was itself reached by a vote of eight to seven, and might easily have gone the other way. Alternatively, the Court in the 1962 case might have reserved its decision on the standing of the applicants, pending an examination of the merits. In such an event, the 1966 decision could have been reached without uncomfortable questions concerning a possible repudiation of the law of the case.

The heart of the matter, as it appears to me, was exposed by the conflict of views between Judges Spender and Fitzmaurice as expressed in their joint dissenting opinion in the 1962 case and Judge Jessup in his separate opinion in the same case. Judges Spender and Fitzmaurice, in their 1962 joint dissenting opinion, had been explicit in their fear lest Article 2 of the mandate involve the Court in a morass of nonjusticiable issues. The draftsmen of the 1966 judg-

ment were less than explicit, but, as I see it, the critical
component in the factors that shaped their decision was a
similar fear.

In the present inquiry, we seek to estimate how far adjudication and quasi-adjudication may be relevant to the settlement of the types of disputes that characterize contemporary
international life. Our scrutiny relates to adjudication as an
institution rather than to particular judgments. In order to
assess the long-range implications of the South West Africa
cases, it is therefore necessary to appraise the judgments and
their consequences not only as they were but also as they
might easily have been. I begin with an examination of the
actual consequences of the actual judgment.

II

The 1966 judgment abandoned the field to whatever
action might be taken by a political organ. In short order,
the General Assembly took the International Court of
Justice at its word and occupied the field. At least, the General Assembly took the Court at what it chose to consider
the Court's word. If the Court regarded the questions as
beyond its reach, the General Assembly would deal with
them. In dealing with them, the General Assembly, as we
shall see, piled ambiguities of its own onto the ambiguities
in the judgment of the Court. When the Court dismissed
the questions, it made clear only its own disinclination to
deal with them. It passed on to whomsoever it might concern a set of interlocking uncertainties. Were the questions

to be decided by political organs? Were the political organs
to decide the questions on the basis of political criteria, or
were they to apply the criteria of the mandate as objectively
as possible? In turning to examine the actions of the General
Assembly, we shall have to consider how far the Assembly
conceived "political" in the sense of relating to policy and
how far in the sense of political opportunism, convenience,
or whim. To the extent that we may find the General Assembly guided by the former meaning of "political," we
shall also have to consider whether the Assembly regarded
the "political" issues as issues of policy to be approached in
the spirit of law.

In its Resolution No. 2145 (XXI) of October 28, 1966,
the General Assembly recalled the three Advisory Opinions
of July 11, 1950, June 7, 1955 and June 1, 1956, as well as
the litigated judgment of December 21, 1962. It expressed
its grave concern "at the situation in the Mandated Territory, which has seriously deteriorated following the judgment of the International Court of Justice of 18 July 1966."
It reaffirmed "that South West Africa is a territory having
international status and that it shall maintain this status
until it achieves independence." It declared "that South
Africa has failed to fulfill its obligations in respect of the
administration of the Mandated Territory and to ensure the
moral and material well-being and security of the indigenous inhabitants of South-West Africa and has, in fact, disavowed the Mandate." Grasping the nettle at its root, it
decided "that the Mandate . . . is therefore terminated, that
South Africa has no other right to administer the Territory
and that henceforth South West Africa comes under the

direct responsibility of the United Nations." It established
the *Ad Hoc* Committee for South West Africa, composed of
fourteen member states, to "recommend practical means by
which South West Africa should be administered, so as to
enable the people of the Territory to exercise the right of
self-determination and to achieve independence, and to report to the General Assembly at a special session as soon as
possible and in any event not later than April 1967."

In Resolution No. 2145 (XXI), the General Assembly
spoke with an almost unanimous voice. One hundred and
fourteen of the one hundred twenty-one member states
voted aye. Only two, Portugal and South Africa itself, voted
nay. Three abstained: the United Kingdom, France, and
Malawi. Two tiny new African states, Botswana and Lesotho, were absent.[1]

On April 21, 1967, the General Assembly convened in its
Fifth Special Session. Two questions dominated the agenda,
the question of South West Africa and the question of
United Nations peacekeeping operations. The fourteen-
member *Ad Hoc* Committee for South West Africa reported.
Unable to achieve agreement within itself, the committee
transmitted three formal proposals. One was a so-called five-
power proposal sponsored by Ethiopia, Nigeria, Senegal,
the United Arab Republic, and Pakistan. One was a so-
called three-power proposal, submitted by Canada, Italy,
and the United States. One was a two-power proposal, sponsored by Chile and Mexico. In the ensuing debate, African
and Asian states rallied behind the five-power proposal.
With some modifications, it was resubmitted as a so-called

1 See footnote, 61 Am. J. Int. L. 649 (April 1967).

African-Asian proposal, sponsored by fifty-six African and Asian states. The other proposals came to be referred to in debate as the Latin American proposal and the Western. After two weeks of interchange on the pros and cons of the respective proposals, discussions were suspended to permit informal consultations looking toward a possible working consensus. The consultations did succeed in resolving the differences between the African-Asian and Latin American submissions. A new draft resolution, sponsored by seventy-nine African, Asian, and Latin American states together with Yugoslavia, was introduced into the General Assembly on May 19, 1967. It was adopted on the same day, as Resolution No. 2248, by a vote of eighty-five in favor and two against (South Africa itself and Portugal), with thirty abstentions.[2]

By its terms, the General Assembly decided to establish a United Nations Council for South West Africa, together with a United Nations Commissioner for South West Africa. The council would "administer South West Africa until independence, with the maximum possible participation of the people of the Territory." It would arrange to hold elections within South West Africa on the basis of universal adult suffrage, through which a legislative assembly would be chosen. Pending the creation of the legislative assembly, the council itself would promulgate any needed laws and would "take all the necessary measures for the maintenance of law and order in the Territory." The United Nations Commissioner for South West Africa would discharge "exec-

2 Gen. Ass. Res. 2248 (S-V), May 19, 1967; A/L.516/Rev. 1 (May 19, 1967). See U.N. Press Release WS/295, May 26, 1967, p. 7; WS/306, Aug. 11, 1967, p. 5; U.N. Monthly Chronicle, vol. IV, no. 6, pp. 27, 36, 112 (June 1967).

utive and administrative tasks" in behalf of the council.
Expenses directly related to the operation of the council and
the commissioner would be met from the regular budget of
the United Nations. The "administration of South West
Africa under the United Nations [would] be financed from
the revenues collected in the Territory." The council would
base itself in South West Africa, and would "proceed to
South West Africa with a view to (a) Taking over the administration of the Territory; (b) Ensuring the withdrawal of
South African police and military forces; (c) Ensuring the
withdrawal of South African personnel and their replacement by personnel operating under the authority of the
Council; [and] (d) Ensuring that in the utilization and re-
cruitment of personnel preference be given to the indigenous people."[3]

The independence of South West Africa remained the
stated goal. The territory was to become independent "on a
date to be fixed in accordance with the wishes of the people,"
and the council was charged with doing all in its power to
bring about independence by June 1968. Promptly upon the
declaration of independence, the council would "transfer
all powers to the people of the Territory."

The resolution called upon South Africa "to facilitate the
transfer of the administration of the Territory of South
West Africa to the Council" and requested the Security
Council "to take all appropriate measures to enable the
United Nations Council for South West Africa to discharge"
its functions.[4]

3 Gen. Ass. Res. 2248 (S-V), May 19, 1967. See also U.N. Monthly Chronicle,
vol. IV, no. 6, pp. 27, 36-37 (June 1967).
4 Gen. Ass. Res. 2248 (S-V), May 19, 1967; U.N. Press Release WS/294, May
19, 1967, pp. 5-6; see WS/295, May 26, 1967, p. 7.

The members of the council would be drawn from eleven nations, elected by the General Assembly. The commissioner would also be chosen by the Assembly on the nomination of the Secretary General.

The Fifth Special Session of the General Assembly came to an end on June 13, 1967. At the final meeting, it elected eleven states as members of the United Nations Council for South West Africa. Two were sub-Saharan African states, Nigeria and Zambia; one was a North African state, the United Arab Republic; three were Asian states, India, Pakistan, and Indonesia; three were Latin American states, Chile, Colombia, and Guiana; one, Turkey, straddled Europe and Asia; and one was European, Yugoslavia. The Secretary General, preoccupied by Middle Eastern concerns, needed more time to submit a definitive nomination of the United Nations Commissioner for South West Africa to the General Assembly. Pending the final selection, Constantine A. Stravropoulos, Legal Counsel of the United Nations, was appointed Acting United Nations Commissioner for South West Africa. The council held its first meeting on August 10, 1967, decided to rotate its presiding officer on a monthly basis, and elected the Chilean member as president for the first month. Deferring further organization of its work until its next meeting, it adjourned *sine die*, subject to call.[5]

At this writing, neither the council nor the commissioner has proceeded "to South West Africa with a view to taking

5 U.N. Press Release WS/309 of September 1, 1967, p. 2, reported: "The United Nations Council for South West Africa has approved the text of a letter to be sent to the Foreign Minister" of South Africa, "drawing his attention to General Assembly resolution 2145 (XXI) . . . and 2248 (S-V) . . . The Council's letter also asks the Foreign Minister to 'indicate the measures that the Government of South Africa proposes to facilitate the transfer of the administration of the Territory [of South West Africa] to it' (GA/3436)."

over the administration of the Territory" and "ensuring the withdrawal of South African police and military forces and . . . personnel and their replacement by personnel operating under the authority of the Council." I do not know when the journey may be undertaken. If the South African army and police should prove inhospitable, questions of law and force may arise.

The original African-Asian draft resolution, sponsored by fifty-six countries, had contained a proposed clause under which any obstruction by South Africa involving a use or threat of force would have been declared "an act of aggression"[6] and "a flagrant defiance of the authority of the United Nations"[7] leading to a request to the Security Council to take enforcement action under Chapter VII of the United Nations Charter. If South Africa should prove obdurate, voices might be raised again in the General Assembly to the same effect. But even if an eventual consensus in favor of drastic action by the United Nations could be assumed— and this would be a considerable assumption—it would remain less than clear whether, how, and in what degree a transition could be effected from clamor to action, given the anxieties of the great powers over other parts of the world. In the vociferous tumult that might ensue, South Africa might challenge the legal validity of Resolution No. 2145 of October 27, 1966, and Resolution No. 2248 of May 19, 1967. It is also possible that questions of law, or even questions of policy touched with a sense of law, might be lost in the shuffle. But the questions would be there, whatever the rug under which they might be swept.

6 U.N. Press Release WS/294, May 19, 1967, p. 6.
7 A/L. 516; see also U.N. Press Release WS/291, April 28, 1967, p. 2.

In Resolution No. 2145, as we have seen, the General Assembly declared that South Africa had failed to meet its obligations under the mandate over South West Africa and had in fact disavowed the mandate. On that ground, the General Assembly pronounced the mandate at an end. Did it have authority to do so?

Under Article 7 of the mandate, the Permanent Court of International Justice was expressly authorized to resolve "any dispute whatever . . . between the Mandatory and another member of the League of Nations relating to the *interpretation or the application* of the provisions of the Mandate" (italics mine). In its advisory opinion of July 11, 1950, the International Court of Justice determined that the mandate remained in effect, that the supervisory functions previously exercised by the Council of the League of Nations had passed to the General Assembly of the United Nations, and that the International Court of Justice had succeeded to the authority of the Permanent Court of International Justice under Article 7 of the mandate. The advisory opinion was accepted by the General Assembly. Whatever moral force might be accorded such an advisory opinion, our earlier analysis demonstrated that the opinion was not binding in law upon any organ of the United Nations or upon any state that did not accept it. Twelve years later, however, the opinion received additional powerful support. It was explicitly affirmed and renewed by the International Court of Justice in the first of the South West Africa Cases, in 1962. Under Article 59 of the Statute of the Court, the 1962 decision, rendered in a contentious proceeding, had binding force between the parties in respect to the particular case. In 1962 then, the continued life of the mandate, the power of the International Court of Justice to interpret it, and the supervisory authority of the General Assembly as successor to the Council of the League stood as authoritatively established for the General Assembly, by virtue of its acceptance of the Advisory Opinion of 1950, and for South Africa, Ethiopia, and Liberia as the parties to the litigated case, for all purposes connected with that case.

A shadow of uncertain darkness was cast over the position by a specially puzzling paragraph in the generally puzzling 1966 South West Africa judgment. Before taking up "the question of the Applicants' standing in the present phase of the proceedings," the Court insisted that "it should be made clear that when, in the present Judgment, the Court considers what provisions of the Mandate for South West Africa involve a legal right or interest for the Applicants, and what not, it does so without pronouncing upon, and wholly without prejudice to, the question of whether that Mandate is still in force. The Court moreover thinks it necessary to state that its 1962 decision on the question of competence was equally given without prejudice to that of the survival of the Mandate, which is a question appertaining to the merits of the case. It was not in issue in 1962, except in the sense that survival had to be assumed for the purpose of determining the purely jurisdictional issue which is all that was then before the Court."[8]

I am at a loss to see how the majority could have reconciled the quoted paragraph with the 1962 judgment. South

8 South West Africa Cases, Second Phase, ICJ Rep. 1966, pp. 6, 18, 19 (July 18, 1966).

Africa, in its first preliminary objection, had explicitly placed in issue its contention that the mandate "had never been and was no longer a treaty or convention in force." In quashing the objection, the Court explicitly reaffirmed the view expressed in the Advisory Opinion of July 11, 1950, that the mandate was "an international agreement having the character of a treaty" and that it survived and remained in effect.[9] It is hard to know to what extent the quoted paragraph might be deemed to impair the effect of the 1962 judgment. It is not hard, however, to imagine an effort by South Africa to make use of it. For our purposes, I note the paragraph as a possible complicating factor, but assume that it vitiated neither the continuing validity and effect of the mandate nor the supervisory functions of the General Assembly under the mandate.

If then it be taken as established that the International Court of Justice had authority to interpret the mandate and determine the application of its provisions, at least in relation to the General Assembly, Ethiopia, Liberia, and South Africa, the fact remains that it declined to do so. As we have seen, the Court left the field to whatever political organ might see fit to occupy it, and the General Assembly moved in to give effect to its supervisory responsibility.

But the existence of such a supervisory responsibility is one thing. Its scope is another. Did the scope embrace authority to determine that South Africa as the mandatory had violated the terms of the mandate to such a degree as to constitute a disavowal warranting a declaration of forfeiture? Nowhere in the language of the mandate or in any

---

9 See above, p. 85.

advisory opinion or judgment of the International Court of
Justice can words be found expressly conferring such an
authority upon the General Assembly, or upon its predeces-
sor in supervisory responsibility, the Council of the League
of Nations. If the authority is to be established, it must be
inferred. It can perhaps be inferred from Article 6 of the
mandate. The mandate in Article 6 required South Africa
to "make to the Council of the League of Nations an annual
report *to the satisfaction of the Council,* containing full
information with regard to the Territory, and indicating
the measures taken *to carry out the obligations assumed* under Article 2, 3, 4 and 5" (italics mine).

Although an inference of the kind here in question may
not come free of difficulties to an objective mind, it is not
analytically excluded. In requiring an annual report *"to
the satisfaction of the Council,"* Article 6 can reasonably
be construed to require that the Council be satisfied not
merely with the form and quantitative adequacy of the report but with the conduct of the mandatory revealed by it,
notably the "measures taken [by the mandatory] *to carry out
the obligations assumed* under Articles 2, 3, 4 and 5" (italics
mine). A stipulation that the Council must be satisfied may
be also taken to imply authority for it to give effect to any
dissatisfaction it may feel, through appropriate steps. But
a more restrictive interpretation could also be rationally supported. Whatever the arguments that might be marshaled
for and against either view, the General Assembly appears
in the main to have ignored them.

The Assembly did explicitly rest its assertion of supervisory power upon the advisory opinions of the International

Court of Justice and the litigated judgment of December 21, 1962. But it bounded lightly over the gulf between a determination that it had some sort of supervisory responsibility and a determination that such responsibility encompassed a power to judge the conduct of the mandatory and to pronounce a forfeiture of the mandate. There is no evidence that it troubled itself to find the source of such an authority in the terms of the mandate. It relied primarily on the record of its own cumulative drive toward the granting of independence to colonial countries and peoples, spearheaded by its own Committee of Twenty-Four, highlighted by its own Resolutions No. 1514 (XV) of December 14, 1960, and No. 1810 (XVII) of December 17, 1962, and supplemented by the Security Council's Resolution No. 183 of July 31, 1963.[10]

Again and again since 1960, the General Assembly had sounded the tocsin to signal "the right [of all peoples] to self-determination" and the duty of all states exercising power over "Non-Self-Governing Territories or all other territories which have not yet attained independence, to transfer all powers to the people of those territories, without any conditions or reservations, in accordance with their freely expressed will and desire, without any distinction as to race, creed or colour."[11] The Assembly's Resolution No. 2145 (XXI) of October 27, 1966, brought its doctrine sharply to focus on South Africa in relation to South West Africa.

A hard-nosed lawyer might wonder whether the General Assembly was seeking to lift itself by its own bootstraps, citing only its own prior declarations as authority to support

10 See above, pp. 58-61.
11 Gen. Ass. Res. 1514 (XV), Dec. 14, 1960.

its current action. His skepticism would be unwarranted to the extent that the prior declarations rested upon a legitimate source of authority. The Assembly's series of resolutions purported to interpret and apply Chapter XI of the United Nations Charter, particularly Article 73. In Chapter 3, we took account of the "inherent" power of the General Assembly to "interpret such parts of the Charter as are applicable to its particular functions." But we also discovered that its interpretations would not necessarily bind any other organ of the United Nations or any member state. It appeared that neither the General Assembly nor the International Court of Justice, nor any other organ of the United Nations, had conclusive authority to interpret the Charter. On the contrary, "if an interpretation made by any organ of the Organization . . . is not generally acceptable it will be without binding force . . . Where it is desired to establish an authoritative interpretation as a precedent for the future, it may be necessary to embody the interpretation in an amendment to the Charter." (See above, pp. 62-63.)

As we have seen, Resolution No. 2145 was carried by a vote of one hundred fourteen to two, with three abstentions and two members absent. Botswana and Lesotho were absent; the United Kingdom, France, and Malawai abstained; and only South Africa and Portugal dissented. Unless "generally acceptable" must be taken to mean "unanimously accepted" (as more than one responsible commentator has suggested),[12] it is conceivable that the vote on Resolution No. 2145 signified a general acceptability. It is conceivable, but "it ain't necessarily so."

---

[12] See, for example, Salo Engel, *Procedures for the de Facto Revision of the Charter*, Proceedings Am. Soc. Int. Law (April 1965), pp. 108, 116.

In my judgment, even if the vote were one hundred twenty to one, with only South Africa dissenting, it would require more than a nose count to establish the binding quality of the interpretation. The process by which each delegate arrived at his vote would be relevant. It would indeed be critical. In the degree to which any delegate's vote might reflect partisan political jockeying, or a personal or national political preference, convenience, or whim, its probative value would be dissipated. It would not in fact be an interpretation at all, in any morally or intellectually meaningful sense. It would be simply a political maneuver. But in the degree to which a delegate's vote represented a conscientious and rational attempt to arrive at an objective appraisal of the meaning of a provision of the Charter in the light of its purposes, it could properly be counted in a calculation of whether the interpretation was "generally acceptable."

Are you troubled by a seeming intimation that the effect of a parliamentary resolution may turn upon an inquiry into the motives and mental processes of the legislators? I have intimated nothing of the sort. The General Assembly of the United Nations is not a parliamentary body, despite rhetorical flourishes that may so describe it. Whether the delegates bear ambassadorial titles or not, they are diplomatic representatives, not parliamentary. They are diplomatic emissaries of a special kind who convene in an assembly for multilateral diplomacy. Like other diplomatic representatives, they are governed by instructions received from the respective foreign offices of the respective governments.

The relevance of the process by which delegates reach a vote to the interpretative significance of their vote may be

related to a fundamental doctrine concerning the sources of
international law. It is familiar learning that the existence
and scope of a rule of international law can be established
by a uniform state practice, if and only if the practice reflects
an opinion of law. In the words of a standard treatise: "Custom is the older and the original source of International
Law . . . Custom must not be confused with usage. In every-
day life and language both terms are used synonymously,
but in the language of the international jurist they have two
distinctly different meanings. International jurists speak of
a *custom* when a clear and continuous habit of doing certain
actions has grown up [among states] under the aegis of the
conviction that these actions are, according to International
Law, obligatory or right. On the other hand, they speak of
a *usage* when a habit of doing certain actions has grown up
without there being the conviction that these actions are,
according to International Law, obligatory or right."[13]
    Another treatise puts the doctrine even more explicitly:
Customary international law has "two constitutive elements: (a) a general practice of States and (b) the acceptance
by States of this general practice as law. It is not sufficient
to show that States follow habitually a certain line of conduct, either in doing or not doing something. In order to
prove the existence of a rule of international customary law,
it is necessary to establish that States act in this way because
they recognize a *legal* obligation to this effect."[14] The doctrine has been concisely incorporated into Clause b of

    13 L. Oppenheim, *International Law*, 8th ed. H. Lauterpacht (London, New
York, and Toronto: Longmans, Green & Co., 1955), I, 25-26.
    14 Georg Schwarzenberger, *A Manual of International Law*, 4th ed. (New
York: Frederick A. Praeger, 1960), I, 27.

Article 38 of the Statute of the International Court of Justice, which enjoins the Court to apply "international custom, as evidence of a general practice accepted as law."

In the *Asylum* case, the International Court of Justice spelled out the doctrine and applied it concretely. Colombia, in a proceeding against Peru, had sought to invoke an alleged rule of customary international law. The Court emphasized that the Colombian government "must prove that the rule invoked by it is in accordance with a constant and uniform usage practised by the States in question, and that this usage is the expression of a right . . . [The] Colombian Government has referred to a large number of particular cases in which diplomatic asylum was in fact granted and respected. But it has not shown that the alleged rule . . . was . . . exercised by the States granting asylum as a right appertaining to them and respected by the territorial States as a duty incumbent on them and not merely for *reasons of political expediency*. The facts brought to the knowledge of the Court disclosed so much uncertainty . . . and the practice has been so much influenced by *considerations of political expediency* in the various cases that it is not possible to discern in all this *any constant and uniform usage, accepted as law*" (italics mine).[15]

We can search the debates in the General Assembly for an indication of how far the votes of the delegates may have reflected an objective appraisal of the meaning of Article 73 of the Charter in relation to South West Africa and how far they may have reflected political preferences or conveniences. It comes as no surprise to discover that the debates

15 Asylum Case (Colombia/Peru), ICJ Rep. 1950, pp. 266, 276-277.

do not clearly illuminate the point. A report of the Special Committee of Twenty-Four launched the proceedings. Through its Subcommittee on South West Africa, the Special Committee deplored the decision of the International Court of Justice to dismiss the case filed by Ethiopia and Liberia "on technical grounds, without adjudicating upon the substance of the matter." It "unanimously condemned South Africa's barbaric administration of the mandated territory and its intransigent attitude despite the innumerable pleas made by the United Nations. It was convinced that South Africa, by its unchanging behaviour, had thoroughly disqualified itself from administering the mandate over the territory."[16]

In the debate, many representatives "expressed the view that an International Mandate was a sacred trust and that the Assembly had the right not only to endow but to revoke a mandate." Many representatives "stressed the need for an effective resolution in order to facilitate the eradication of colonialism and *apartheid* and to fulfil the obligations of the United Nations . . . The decision of the International Court of Justice of July 18 [1966] was severely criticised by many speakers; several representatives however stressed that the United Nations recommendations must be in accordance with sound legal principles. Speaking along these lines were representatives of Brazil, New Zealand and Australia and France. The representative of France stated that the Mandate had survived after the dissolution of the League, but the substitution of the United Nations for the League did not give members of the Organization more competence

16 U.N. Monthly Chronicle, vol. III, no. 9, p. 27 (October 1966).

than the League had exercised. France had doubts about the legal basis of the proposals in the draft resolution."[17] The representative of Algeria objected to a proposed sub-amendment offered by the United States because it "opened the risk of bringing a question which the United Nations had decided to deal with politically back into the legal sphere." The representative of Tanzania "hoped the United States would cooperate by withdrawing its sub-amendment, especially as the support of the permanent members of the Security Council for the draft was so essential." The representative of the United Kingdom felt that "the draft resolution would have certain defects, and his delegation had serious reservations about it. The words 'including the right to revert to itself the administration of the Mandated Territory,' in the last paragraph of the preamble, were a clause which his delegate regarded as doubtful in law and as stating a conclusion which the United Kingdom thought the Assembly would be unwise to reach. The Assembly should not at this stage do more than state that South Africa's rights under the Mandate had been terminated." The Netherlands representative emphasized the anxiety of his delegation "that the Organization should not approve resolutions it could not carry out." The representative of Guinea "considered that the United States sub-amendment contains several dangerous elements. The United Nations should lead the people of South West Africa to independence. He hoped all the great powers—the United States, the Soviet Union and the United Kingdom—would join in the move to enable South West Africans to exercise their rights of self-determination."

17 U.N. Monthly Chronicle, vol. III, no. 10, pp. 20-21 (November 1966).

The representative of Italy "said his delegation had voted for the resolution because it was the result of a great deal of give and take." The representative of Belgium "said his delegation's support of the resolution was not without reservations." The Australian representative "said it was not clear what would follow from the resolution," although he supported it. The representative of the United States, after voting for the resolution, indicated that "his delegation would have preferred a wider consensus, including the support of all permanent members of the Security Council."

The French representative, explaining his abstention, emphasized that although France "did not exclude a policy of revoking the Mandate, it could not agree to the manner in which it was proposed that this should be done, as reflected in the resolution. His delegation disagreed with the reference to resolution 1514 (XV). The special case of South West Africa had nothing to gain by a text of so doubtful a nature." The representative of the U.S.S.R. "said his delegation had voted for the resolution in support of the African people's struggle against racists and their protectors, although it considered that the amendments had weakened the original draft . . . His delegation had voted against the United States sub-amendment because it considered that it was intended to render the resolution null and void . . . [his government] opposed paragraph 9 in the original resolution, which had given the Secretary General unlimited financial and administrative power in South West Africa. This was against the provisions of the Charter . . . The experience of the Congo constrained his delegation to reserve its position on the paragraph."[18]

18 U.N. Monthly Chronicle, vol. III, no. 10, pp. 23-27 (November 1966).

In sum, only the French representative appeared to be
concerned to find a source of authority in the terms of the
mandate itself. Doubting his capacity to do so, he reminded
his colleagues that the powers of the General Assembly over
the mandate could rise no higher than those of the League
of Nations. He regretted the reference to Resolution No.
1514 (XV) as irrelevant and confusing. The representatives
of Brazil, Australia, New Zealand, and the United Kingdom
also expressed legal worries but did not make their nature
explicit. The Algerian delegate proclaimed with apparent
satisfaction a shift of the United Nations from the legal
sphere into the political; and the representatives of the
Soviet Union added a blast against "racists and their protectors." For the rest, the varied comments of the delegates
leave a net impression that they were following the line
drawn by the General Assembly from Article 73 of the
Charter through Resolutions No. 1514 (XV) and No. 1810
(XVII) to Resolution No. 2145 (XXI), possibly taking for
granted, without re-examination, that the resolutions were
authorized by Article 73, or more broadly by Chapters XI,
XII, and XIII of the Charter, or perhaps by Article 10.

On this record, not even a soft-nosed lawyer could find the
one hundred and fourteen votes in favor of Resolution No.
2145 to reflect one hundred and fourteen carefully considered opinions, reached through rational analysis, that Article 73 of the Charter authorized the General Assembly to
cancel a mandate under Article 22 of the Covenant of the
League of Nations. The one hundred and fourteen votes
(out of a General Assembly membership of a hundred and
twenty one) do not represent a "generally acceptable interpretation" of the Charter. A foundation in law for the

authority of the General Assembly to cancel the mandate
has not yet been established.

I do not say that such a validation could not have been
effected nor that it may not yet be. Of alternative possibilities, more later. But I do suggest that a validation in law
cannot be based on the course of events in the General Assembly up to the time of this writing.

As a practical matter, how might the question of the lawful authority of the General Assembly to cancel the mandate
come up? Suppose the United Nations Council and Commissioner for South West Africa should proceed to the territory to give effect to Resolution No. 2248 (S-V) of May
19, 1967. They would try to begin "Taking over the administration of the Territory, Ensuring the withdrawal of South
African police and military forces, [and] Ensuring the withdrawal of South African personnel and their replacement by
[preferably indigenous] personnel operating under" the
Council's authority. Conceivably, South Africa might acquiesce. Realistically, South Africa might be expected to resist.
It is of some interest to conjecture on what grounds South
Africa might attempt to justify its resistance.

Would South Africa repeat its earlier contention that the
mandate had lapsed? If so, would it assert that it had some-
how acquired sovereignty? Would it protest in the alternative that, in any event, it occupied the territory as a mandatory power under the still valid mandate? Whatever its
hypothesis, it would presumably denounce Resolutions No.
2248 and No. 2145 as unlawful. We may assume that the
General Assembly would again censure South Africa and
insist on the validity of its own resolutions and actions. The

Assembly and South Africa might swing into a renewed cycle of assertion and counterassertion.

Following intimations in the debates leading up to the adoption of Resolution No. 2248 and in the text of the resolution itself,[19] the General Assembly might call on the Security Council for support. Such a call would presumably invoke enforcement action under Chapter VII of the Charter, on a theory that South African obduracy amounted to a "threat to the peace, breach of the peace, or act of aggression." South Africa might be expected to return the compliment, branding the General Assembly as the aggressor, and pleading that it was merely defending its lawful occupancy against an unlawful encroachment by a self-styled United Nations Council and Commissioner for South West Africa.

So the question of the validity in law of Resolution No. 2145 might arise, in a way that would foster neither a clarification of the issues nor an orderly disposition. But it might have an effect, nagging at the minds of politicians and officials and, in nations in which public opinion counts, at the minds of the citizenry. The effect might suffice to tip the balance in the Security Council toward inaction.

[19] See pp. 108, 110 and notes 4, 6, 7. On November 10, 1967, the United Nations Council for South West Africa reported that South Africa's obduracy made it "impossible for the Council to discharge effectively all of the functions and responsibilities entrusted to it by the Assembly." It considered "that the continued presence of South African authorities in South West Africa constitutes an illegal act, a usurpation of power and a foreign occupation of the territory which seriously threaten international peace and security." In these circumstances, it recommended that the General Assembly request "appropriate action" by the Security Council in accordance with paragraph 5 of section IV of Gen. Ass. Res. 2248 (S-V). See A/6897, Nov. 10, 1967; U.N. Press Release WS/320, Nov. 17, 1967, p. 9.

The members of the Security Council have other problems of their own. The permanent members, on whom the burden of enforcement would primarily fall, are confronted by multiple acute demands upon their attention and resources. States do not ordinarily welcome external invitations to use their armed forces to serve purposes other than their own vital national interests which they believe to be under an immediate and serious threat. Adherence to the Charter of the United Nations does imply an enlarged conception of national purposes. Signatory states in effect agree to regard acts of aggression and breaches of the peace in violation of the Charter as threats to their own vital interests. But it does not impugn the fidelity of states to such an agreement to recognize that they may feel the drag of the old habitual outlook when invited to commit their armed forces to battle. For the permanent members, moreover, the agreement is tempered in principle by the voting procedure in the Security Council that safeguards their ultimate independence of decision. Even in a case in which it might appear relatively clear to informed and responsible men that the conduct of a state amounts to aggression, that such conduct violates identified provisions of the Charter, and that the obligations of the members are engaged, the United States, the Soviet Union, Britain, and France might exhibit no eagerness to muster collective United Nations forces in a common armed endeavor. In the degree to which the occurrence of events alleged to constitute a violation might be uncertain, or the nature of the conduct of an allegedly offending state might be obscure, or the scope and meaning of pertinent provisions of the Charter might be equivocal, the permanent members—and others—might be all the more prone to revert to the customary attitude.

In the South West Africa cases, the withdrawal by the International Court of Justice from the field and the mode of withdrawal left the international community to cope with legal confusion. The behavior of the General Assembly in occupying the field has done little to mitigate the confusion. Unless it can be relieved, it will weigh against the possibility of effective implementation of Resolutions No. 2145 and No. 2248.

I turn now to a speculative appraisal of what the consequences of the judgment in the second South West Africa case might have been if the one-vote margin had swung the other way. I do so for reasons previously explained, which it may be well to repeat. I attempt in these chapters to assess how far and in what way adjudication may be relevant to the settlement of Cold War disputes, and disputes between modern industrial states and newly emerging states or peoples "that have not yet attained a full measure of self-government."[20] We have taken the struggle over the territory of South West Africa in the General Assembly and the Security Council and in the International Court of Justice as illustrative of the latter kind of dispute. Our focus is upon long-term implications discernible in the adjudicated cases. Our concern is therefore with the range of possible decisions realistically available to the Court and not merely with particular results actually reached.

20 See U.N. Charter, Art. 73.

III

Each of the seven dissenting judges explicitly rejected the view of the majority denying standing to the applicants for an asserted want of a "legal right or interest . . . in the subject matter of the present claims." Five—Wellington Koo, the Vice President of the Court, and Judges Tanaka, Padilla Nervo, and Forster, and Judge *Ad Hoc* Mbanefo—discussed and in some degree expressed an opinion on the merits. Judge Koretsky confined his dissent to the point of the majority holding. Judge Jessup, avoiding an actual statement of his view on the merits, suggested lines along which the merits could and should have been analyzed and intimated what his view might have been.

Judge Koretsky dissented "because the Court reverts in essence to its Judgment of 21 December 1962 on the same cases and in fact revises it even without observing Article 61[21] of the Statute and without the procedure envisaged in Article 78[22] of the Rules of Court."[23] Apart from the law of the case, Judge Koretsky made clear his conviction that the 1962 judgment had been correct. In his opinion, the applicants "have laid before the Court the question of how to interpret the provisions of the Mandate; whether they are rightly

---

21 Art. 61 provides: "An application for revision of a judgment may be made only when it is based upon the discovery of some fact of such a nature as to be a decisive factor, which fact was, when the judgment was given, unknown to the Court and also to the party claiming revision . . ."

22 Under Art. 78 of the Rules of the Court, a "request for the revision of a judgment shall be made by an application. The application . . . shall contain the particulars necessary to show that the conditions laid down by Article 61 of the Statute are fulfilled."

23 South West Africa Cases, Second Phase, ICJ Rep. 1966, pp. 6, 239 (July 18, 1966).

applied by the Mandatory; whether the Mandatory's policy in the Territory of South West Africa, which has caused so much concern to world public opinion and to Members of the United Nations, is consistent with the provisions of the Mandate."[24]

In whatever measure the several dissenting opinions reached beyond the question of standing to the merits, all concentrated upon the third and fourth of the applicants' submissions. Although the general tenor of the submissions had been maintained since the filing of the applications, changes had been made in the numerical sequence and especially in the language of two that derived from the second paragraph of Article 2 of the mandate. In their final revision, the two submissions, numbered 3 and 4, read:

> (3) Respondent, by laws and regulations, and official methods and measures, which are set out in the pleadings herein, has practiced apartheid, i.e., has distinguished as to race, colour, national or tribal origin in establishing the rights and duties of the inhabitants of the Territory; that such practice is in violation of its obligations as stated in Article 2 of the Mandate and Article 22 of the Covenant of the League of Nations; and that Respondent has the duty forthwith to cease the practice of apartheid in the Territory;

> (4) Respondent, by virtue of economic, political, social and educational policies applied within the Territory, by means of laws and regulations, and official methods and measures, which are set out in the plead-

24 *Ibid.,* p. 248.

ings herein, has, in the light of applicable international standards or international legal norm [*sic*], or both, failed to promote to the utmost the material and moral well-being and social progress of the inhabitants of the Territory; that its failure to do so is in violation of its obligations as stated in Article 2 of the Mandate and Article 22 of the Covenant; and that Respondent has the duty forthwith to cease its violations as aforesaid and to take all practicable action to fulfill its duties under such Articles.[25]

These were submissions of a kind that in 1962 had filled Judges Spender and Fitzmaurice with foreboding, lest they draw the Court into "questions of appreciation rather than of objective determination," appropriate for a political or technical forum but lying beyond the proper sphere of judicial determination.[26]

But the dissenting judges, although acknowledging the depth and intricacy of the issues, did not find them judicially unmanageable. In the opinion of Judge Tanaka, "the Court should proceed to decide the questions of the 'ultimate' merits which have arisen from the Applicants' final submissions." While the Court "cannot examine and pronounce the legality or illegality of the policy of apartheid as a whole, it can decide that there exist some elements in the apartheid policy which are not in conformity with the principle of equality before the law or international standard or international norm of non-discrimination and non-separation." Al-

25 *Ibid.*, pp. 15, 284, 444-445.
26 See above, pp. 94-95.

though legislation could reasonably take account of differences in sex, age, or language, "Discrimination according to the criterion of 'race, colour, national or tribal origin' in establishing the rights and duties of the inhabitants of the territory is not considered reasonable and just." In consequence, "the Applicants' Submissions Nos. 3 and 4 are well-founded."[27] With less elaboration and precision, Judges Wellington Koo, Padilla Nervo, Forster, and Mbanefo reached comparable conclusions.[28]

Refraining from a definite pronouncement on the merits, Judge Jessup projected a pattern that he believed proper and desirable for an analysis of the issues raised by the applicants' third and fourth submissions. He distinguished two aspects of the applicants' case, one "based on the argument of the existence of a norm as a rule of law and the other . . . on a standard of interpretation to which the governing effect of a legal rule was not attributed."[29] In the first aspect, as Judge Jessup discerned it, the applicants seemed to contend that the conduct of South Africa had violated a

> so-called norm of non-discrimination [which] had become a rule of international law through reiterated statements and resolutions of the General Assembly, of the International Labour Organization and of other international bodies. Such a contention would be open to a double attack: first, that since these international bodies lack a true legislative character, their resolutions

27 South West Africa Cases, Second Phase, ICJ Rep. 1966, pp. 6, 250, 315, 314, 316 (July 18, 1966).
28 Ibid., p. 235 (Wellington Koo); p. 464, but cf. pp. 460-461 (Padilla Nervo); pp. 482-483 (Forster); p. 490 (Mbanefo).
29 Ibid., p. 432.

alone cannot create law; and second, that if Applicants'
case rested upon the thesis that apartheid should be
declared illegal because it conflicted with a general rule
of international law, it might be questioned whether
such a claim would fairly fall within the ambit of
paragraph 2 of Article 7 . . . of the Mandate. If the
Court were to hold that the practice of apartheid is a
violation of a general rule (norm) of international law,
it might seem to be passing on the legality of acts per-
formed within the Republic of South Africa itself, a
matter which, as already noted, would be outside the
Court's jurisdiction. On the other hand, if the Court
had considered the question of the existence of an international standard or criterion as an aid to interpretation of the Mandate, it would have been pursuing a
course to which no objection could be raised. In my
opinion, such a standard exists and could have been
and should have been utilized by the Court in perform-
ing what would then be seen as the purely judicial
function of measuring by an objective standard whether
the practice of apartheid in the mandated territory of
South West Africa was a violation of the Mandatory's
obligation to "promote to the utmost the material and
moral well-being and the social progress of the inhabitants of the territory."[30]

While Judge Jessup "plainly stated" his unwillingness to
"rest upon the thesis that resolutions of the General Assembly . . . create new rules of law," he regarded an "accumula-

30 *Ibid.*, pp. 432-433.

tion of expressions of condemnation of apartheid . . . especially as recorded in the resolutions of the General Assembly . . . [as] proof of the pertinent contemporary international community standard."[31]

Judge Jessup did not underestimate the complexity of the duties assumed by the mandatory under the second paragraph of Article 2. Necessarily, the mandatory must be allowed latitude in the selection of ways and means. "But the choices of policies followed by a mandatory are subject to review."[32] He posed a hypothetical situation that is charged with possible implications for a possible future course of action in the General Assembly and in the International Court of Justice. Suppose, he suggested, that the League of Nations had remained in existence and that the Permanent Mandates Commission had "continued to function with the same type of expert personnel. Assume that either by receipt of a request from the Council [of the League] for an advisory opinion or by an application filed by a member of the League, the International Court was faced by the question whether the practice of apartheid in South West Africa in 1960 promoted the progress and welfare, etc., of all the inhabitants. Suppose the Court acting under Article 50 of the Statute asked the Permanent Mandates Commission to enquire and give an expert opinion on that question. I suggest that the Commission would have replied that although in 1925 they might not have considered the apartheid policy incompatible with the obligations of the Mandatory under the conditions and circumstances of that era, they now be-

31 *Ibid.*, p. 441.
32 *Ibid.*, p. 434.

lieved that it was incompatible under the conditions of 1960. I believe the Court would have decided that this opinion was well-founded."[33]

In the concluding paragraph of his dissenting opinion, Judge Jessup not only reiterated his conviction that the applicants had the necessary legal interest to give them standing to maintain the proceeding and that the Court should have proceeded to judgment on the merits, but added "that the task of passing upon the Applicants' third submission which asserts that the practice of apartheid is in violation of the Mandatory's obligations as stated in Article 2 of the Mandate and Article 22 of the Covenant of the League of Nations, is a justiciable issue, not just a political question."[34]

The several dissenting opinions, taken in relation to the issues defined by the parties' submissions, indicate the range of reasonable choices within the sphere of judicial decision open to the Court. In going forward to a judgment on the merits, the Court would have automatically reaffirmed its power and duty to interpret the mandate. It would have left standing, or explicitly confirmed, the declarations in its 1962 judgment that the mandate continued in effect and that the General Assembly had succeeded to the supervisory responsibility previously vested in the Council of the League of Nations. It could have taken the applicants' sixth, seventh, and eighth submissions in stride. In the sixth, the applicant asked the Court to find that South Africa had established military bases within the Territory; in the seventh, that South Africa had failed to file and must file annual reports

[33] *Ibid.,* p. 438.
[34] *Ibid.,* p. 442.

with the General Assembly; and in the eighth, that South Africa had failed to transmit and must transmit to the General Assembly petitions from the inhabitants of the Territory. These submissions defined specific issues, well within the sphere of judicial action even narrowly conceived. From comments on the evidence that occur in the dissenting opinions, it appears probable that the Court would have ruled against the applicants on the sixth, but in their favor on the seventh and eighth.

The core issues were raised by the third and fourth submissions of the applicants and the respondent's denial. South Africa had met the third and fourth submissions of Ethiopia and Liberia head on: "(b) Relative to Applicants' submissions numbers 3, 4, 5, 6 and 9, . . . the Respondent has not, in any of the respects alleged, violated its obligations as stated in the Mandate or in Article 22 of the Covenant of the League of Nations."[35] On these issues, the Court might have gone as far as Judge Tanaka, or followed the course projected by Judge Jessup, or stopped short of either.

With Judge Tanaka (and Judges Wellington Koo, Padilla Nervo, Forster, and Mbanefo), the Court might have declared apartheid, as practiced by the respondent in South West Africa, to violate a right to equal protection of the law, deemed by Judge Tanaka a norm of international law. In Judge Tanaka's terms, the Court could have held the vindication of this right to be "a necessary prerequisite of the material and moral well-being and the social progress of the inhabitants of the Territory."[36] It would accordingly have

35 *Ibid.,* p. 17.
36 *Ibid.,* p 315.

equated a breach of the norm with a violation of Article 2 of the mandate.

Judge Jessup's analysis offered a more likely position at which the divisions within the Court might have come to equilibrium. South Africa itself, on occasions during the oral proceedings, had purported to avow that unfair discrimination would violate Article 2 of the mandate. It had protested, however, that apartheid represented a differentiation that was justified, indeed required, by the actual conditions in South West Africa.[37] Its language was not unrelated to the familiar terms of American constitutional doctrine concerning reasonable classification and discrimination under the Fifth and Fourteenth Amendments. To whatever extent these occasional contentions reflected the authentic South African view, they would support Judge Jessup's call for an appraisal based on the facts in the light of a "pertinent contemporary international community standard." Data were available in abundance, gathered through the years by the Permanent Mandates Commission under the League, and the Committee on South West Africa, the Good Offices Committee and other committees of the General Assembly. If need be, the data could be supplemented. Under Article 50 of the Statute of the Court, the Court "may, at any time, entrust any individual, body, bureau, commission, or other organization that it may select, with the task of carrying out an enquiry or giving an expert opinion." A judgment based

---

[37] Cf. Judge Tanaka's reference to the South African argument, in South West Africa Cases, Second Phase, ICJ Rep. 1966, pp. 307-308, 310-312 (July 18, 1966); see Anthony d'Amato, "Legal and Political Strategies of the South West Africa Litigation," *Law in Transition Quarterly*, vol. IV, no. 1 (March 1967), pp. 36-37.

on such an appraisal would be confined in its reach to the application of Article 2 of the mandate to the actual facts and circumstances of South-West Africa during the period surveyed.

Such an appraisal would have to take account of the degree of discretion vested in the mandatory. As Judge Jessup recognized, the mandatory must be accorded flexibility in the discharge of its responsibilities. He insisted that the exercise of discretion was subject to review. Review of what scope? How much weight must the Court give to the mandatory's own judgment? Here the Court might part company with Judge Jessup and go on another tack. It might hold that the discretion vested in the mandatory was so broad as to be reviewable only for possible abuses of discretion. An abuse of discretion would consist of conduct so severely at odds with the outlook and standards of reasonable men in the contemporary world community as to be arbitrary or capricious.

Conceivably, the Court might decide that the mandatory's discretion could be challenged only for bad faith. The Court might even hold the discretion to be absolute, at least in the sense that it was beyond judicial review, whatever political supervision might be exercised by other organs of the United Nations. In effect, such a holding would amount to a determination that questions concerning the propriety of the mandatory's conduct under Article 2 were political and not justiciable. Even such a decision would not quite whip the devil around the stump, restoring the position created by the 1966 judgment. The Court would at least have acknowledged the right of the applicants to bring the proceeding, the continuing validity of the mandate, the supervisory responsibilities of the General Assembly, and its own power and duty to construe the mandate. The way would not have been barred to continuing evolution of the function of the Court. As American lawyers know from American judicial experience, questions deemed political by the courts at one time may be found justiciable at a later time.

Whichever of the foregoing possibilities of decision might have been adopted by the Court, it would have entailed consequences different from those that followed the 1966 judgment.

If the Court were to have adopted the views of Judge Tanaka, South Africa would have been adjudged in violation of Article 2 of the mandate as well as Article 6, requiring it to report to the General Assembly. The judgment would have been declaratory in nature. The applicants had asked for no more. The judgment would have "adjudged and declared" that South Africa as the mandatory power remained subject to the "international obligations stated . . . in the Mandate," that it had violated certain of these obligations, and that it had "the duty forthwith to cease its violations as aforesaid and to take all practicable action to fulfill its duties."[38] The Court would have issued no process. It would have sought to impose no sanctions. But the reciprocal rights and duties, and rights and wrongs, would have been proclaimed by an authoritative tribunal in a judgment binding on the parties under Article 59 of the Statute of the Court. The effect would have been magnified

---

[38] See the applicants' submissions as presented at the hearing on May 19, 1965, especially the opening paragraph and paragraphs (2), (3), and (4). South West Africa Cases, Second Phase, ICJ Rep. 1966, pp. 6, 15-16.

by Article 94 of the Charter, under which "Each Member of the United Nations undertakes to comply with the decision of the International Court of Justice in any case to which it is a party." In the event of its failure "to perform the obligations incumbent upon it under [the] judgment . . . , the other party may have recourse to the Security Council, which may, if it deems necessary, make recommendations or decide upon measures to be taken to give effect to the judgment." A specific basis would have been provided for possible enforcement action by the Security Council, quite apart from any question of acts of aggression, breaches of the peace or threats to the peace under Chapter VII of the Charter. It would not have been plain sailing. The members of the Security Council, especially the permanent members, would have had to evaluate the potential cost to them in blood, treasure, and diplomatic posture in relation to their commitments under the Charter. But the setting for possible action by them would have been more propitious than it would be in the event of a call upon the Security Council by the General Assembly of the kind explored earlier in the present chapter.

The setting would also have been more propitious in the General Assembly. At the very least, the minds of the delegates would have been less heated by resentment and frustration, and a cool and rational analysis of the relevant factors would have been fostered. If South Africa remained obdurate, the General Assembly might have assayed the possibility of basing a declaration of forfeiture on Article 6 of the mandate.[39] It could have examined the data through a com-

39 For the text and an analysis of Art. 6 of the mandate, see above, p. 114.

mittee selected for the purpose. The data would have included whatever facts were contained within reports by
South Africa under Article 6 of the mandate, the volumi-
nous additional reports gathered through the years, and the
judgment of the International Court of Justice itself. From
the examination, the Assembly could have found that the
conduct of the mandatory, and notably the "measures taken
to carry out the obligations assumed under Articles 2, 3, 4
and 5" were unsatisfactory to the General Assembly, in the
exercise of its supervisory responsibility as successor to the
Council of the League. It could have found that the requirements of Article 6 implied an authority on the part of the
General Assembly to give effect to its dissatisfaction through
appropriate steps, and that, in the circumstances, appropriate steps required a cancellation of the mandate. Before
taking definitive action along these lines, it could have submitted its views to the International Court of Justice in the
form of a question on which it sought an advisory opinion.

If the advisory opinion were favorable, it would come in
regular course before the General Assembly for acceptance.
In such a context, it is not impossible that the states which
abstained from voting on Resolution No. 2145 might join
their brethren in accepting the advisory opinion. The vote
might well be one hundred and nineteen to two, with only
South Africa and presumably Portugal opposed. I remain
mindful that an advisory opinion as such would not be
binding upon South Africa. However, a vote of one hundred
nineteen to two, supporting an advisory opinion of the
Court, and related to a systematic review of the relevant
data, would perhaps amount to a "generally acceptable"

interpretation of the Charter. In any event, both a consensus of professional opinion and the common sense of mankind would recognize that a foundation in law had been established on a tenable if not a conclusive basis for a resolution of the General Assembly cancelling the mandate. If the advisory opinion were negative, recourse under Article 94 of the Charter would remain available.

What if the Court were to have aligned itself with Judge Jessup's analysis rather than Judge Tanaka's? It would have undertaken a systematic appraisal of the data, perhaps with expert assistance invoked under Article 50 of its Statute. If the appraisal led it to a judgment that all or some of the practices lumped together under the rubric of apartheid violated Article 2 of the mandate, the judgment would have effects similar to those following a Tanaka-type judgment.

I pass over the third and fourth possibilities of decision previously outlined (that the mandatory's conduct could be reviewed only for a possible abuse of discretion or for bad faith) to consider the last—and most limited—as a point of departure. This would be a judgment reaffirming the continuing effect of the mandate, the supervisory responsibility of the General Assembly, and the power and duty of the Court to construe the mandates; ruling, presumably favorably, on Submissions 7 and 8 of the applicant concerning annual reports and the transmittal of petitions by South Africa; and holding that South Africa, although bound to "promote to the utmost the material and moral well-being and the social progress of the inhabitants" of South West Africa under Article 2 of the mandate, was free to do so through whatever ways and means it deemed appropriate in its discretion, which was not subject to review by the Court. In such an eventuality, the Court would not have withdrawn from the field. The judgment would bind South Africa to resume the filing of annual reports and the transmittal of petitions. If South Africa violated the judgment, Article 94 of the Charter could be invoked. If South Africa complied, the reports and petitions would add to the data available for scrutiny by the General Assembly in determining how far it might be satisfied or dissatisfied under Article 6 of the mandate. The psychological consequences of such a judgment even in respect of Article 2 of the mandate might well have been less devastating than those following the 1966 judgment, and the prospects for cool and carefully considered action in the General Assembly correspondingly improved.

IV

I want to re-emphasize the frame of reference within which I have projected the foregoing speculative analysis. My primary purpose is neither to engage in a critique of the South West Africa cases, nor to mourn what might have been. The critique is incidental to my objective. My concern is with the institutional possibilities of international adjudication, together with what I have called international quasi-adjudication,[40] in relation to the major types of disputes that typify the rough side of contemporary international life.

I have suggested five possibilities of decision within the scope of choices realistically available to the International

40 See above, pp. 36, 104, 127.

Court of Justice in the second South West Africa Case. You may prefer to reject some, or add others. I have forecast some probable consequences. Among these, you may find some persuasive, and others not. I have ventured the forecasts in illustrative, not literal, terms. Without pressing any detail, I do believe that a valid conclusion emerges from the analysis taken as a whole.

Whatever the 1966 judgment in the South West Africa cases may have done for the time being to the role of the International Court of Justice, the institutional potentialities of adjudication by the Court—and international adjudication generally—are relevant to the settlement of the South West Africa dispute and the class of disputes that it exemplifies. The designation of such controversies as disputes "between established states and non-self-governing peoples," drawn from Chapter XI of the Charter, is imprecise, as the South-West Africa cases demonstrate. The cases involve a compound controversy between South Africa and the indigenous inhabitants of the territory of South West Africa, between South Africa and the other African states, and between South Africa and the organized international community as represented first by the Council of the League of Nations and then by the General Assembly and Security Council of the United Nations.

It is the survival of the particular mandate and the terms of the mandate that make international adjudication relevant in the South West Africa cases. Would international adjudication be relevant also to disputes that might arise under trusteeships effective under Chapter XII of the Charter? To disputes that might occur in the absence of a trusteeship or mandate between states "which have . . . responsibilities for the administration of territories whose peoples have not yet attained a full measure of self-government"[41] and the non-self-governing peoples in such territories?

In the following chapter, I shall consider these questions. Before doing so, I shall try to isolate the factors that may explain the difference between the function of international adjudication in such disputes and its function—or lack of function—in Cold War disputes.

[41] U.N. Charter, Art. 73.

CHAPTER SIX

THE LIMITS OF

ADJUDICATION AND

THE SENSE OF LAW

I

Earlier I put forward a view of the optimum conditions for adjudication, and projected a range of variations in which the conditions would become progressively less favorable until the limits of adjudication were reached. In the analysis, Cold War disputes typically fell beyond the limits. We have just seen that disputes of the class exemplified by the South West Africa cases fall within the limits. It remains to trace the bounds of the class. I shall try to do so in the second part of the present chapter. At this point, I want to attempt a diagnosis, to see what differentiates disputes of the South West Africa type from Cold War disputes in terms of their ultimate amenability to adjudication.

"Ultimate amenability" connotes the limits of adjudication in a fundamental sense, in contrast to limits which may be defined for particular tribunals by particular constitutional or statutory provisions.[1] I derive my notion of the

[1] See above, p. 34.

nature and limits of adjudication from the historic experience of the established legal systems best known to us—the common law of England, the United States and the Commonwealth of Nations and the civil law of Continental Europe, Latin America, and those states of Asia and Africa to which it has spread. There are legal systems other than the common law and the civil law, of course. Apart from prior usage, the imagination can invent new terms or new meanings for old terms. Nevertheless, several factors warrant taking the common law and the civil law as the sources for our concept of adjudication in the present context. The basic concepts and modes of thought of international law stem largely from the same roots as the civil law. The most ardent and persuasive advocates of the use of adjudication to settle international disputes—indeed, all with whom I happen to be familiar—draw their supporting data and argumentation from the experience of the civil law and the common law.

The international tribunals available for possible adjudication are identical for Cold War controversies and conflicts of the South West Africa kind. The emotions of the parties are deeply engaged in both, and the issues in both are such that the parties do or readily can regard them as vital. In both, the "real parties in interest," to borrow a term from American legal practice, may include more than the states in the forefront of the controversy. We have noted that the dispute in the South West Africa cases lay only in part between South Africa and Ethiopia and Liberia. It took place also between South Africa and the indigenous inhabitants of South West Africa; between South Africa and the other

African states; and between South Africa and the organized international community. So the United States, in supporting the abortive Bay of Pigs invasion, looked beyond Cuba to the Soviet Union; and American apprehensions concerning Communist China pervade the struggle in Vietnam.

There is one distinction, however, between the two classes of dispute that is conspicuous and critical. It relates to the principles and standards available to be applied in an effort to adjudicate. In Cold War disputes, as we have seen, the principles and standards purportedly available as a guide to peaceful settlement boil down to the objective of peaceful settlement itself.[2] A reiteration that peaceful settlement is a goal does not afford a standard by which to reach it. In the South West Africa dispute, the second paragraph of Article 2 of the mandate and Article 22 of the Covenant of the League provided such a standard. The standard had been established by the common consent of the states concerned. The express agreement of South Africa to the mandate, including Article 2, had been the explicit and indispensable condition for designating it as the mandatory. Although the terms of the standard—"promote to the utmost the material and moral well-being and the social progress of the inhabitants"—if taken by themselves, were broad enough to provide abundant room for doubts, they did not stand by themselves. They were sustained and clarified by a context. The context covered more than the legislative history of Article 22 of the Covenant of the League and Article 2 of the mandate. It comprehended the insistent thrust of colonial peoples toward independence in the course of the twentieth

2 See above, p. 38.

century, the evolving policies of imperial powers toward
granting independence, and a growing international consensus that in time found expression in Chapters XI and
XII of the United Nations Charter.

II

In a dispute arising under a trusteeship agreement made
pursuant to Chapter XII of the Charter, the terms of the
agreement would determine how far our analysis of justiciability in the South West Africa cases might be pertinent
to the dispute. Suppose, for example, that South Africa had
seen fit to place the territory of South West Africa under
the trusteeship system. By Article 79 of the Charter, the
terms of the trusteeship would "be agreed upon by the states
directly concerned, including the mandatory power in the
case of territories held under mandate." Under Article 81,
the trusteeship agreement would "include the terms under
which the trust territory will be administered and designate
the authority which will exercise the administration of the
trust territory."

Assume that the new trusteeship agreement would have
incorporated the language of the old mandate verbatim, except for such obvious minimal changes as the substitution of
"trustee" for "mandatory," "General Assembly" for "Council of the League of Nations," "member of the United
Nations" for "member of the League of Nations" and "International Court of Justice" for "Permanent Court of International Justice." In a proceeding instituted by Ethiopia and

Liberia against South Africa in the International Court of Justice under such a trusteeship agreement, the posture of the parties and the nature of the issues would have been similar to those in the actual South West Africa cases. If not altogether identical, they would have been sufficiently alike to cause a parallel alignment among the judges.

Distinctions could be drawn. The majority could not have raised the ghost of a question concerning the continuing validity and effect of the mandate. Judge Jessup's invocation in his dissenting opinion of "the pertinent contemporary international community standard"[3] as a guide for the interpretation of the trusteeship agreement would have been reinforced by Article 76 of the Charter.[4] But, as I have already suggested, the distinctions would probably not have sufficed to change the alignment of the judges; and the long-range implications would have been in essence the same.

It may be harder to extend the implications of the South West Africa cases to disputes under Article 73 of the Charter than to controversies under trusteeship agreements. Earlier, we touched on a conflict affecting Portugal and Portuguese Angola. Here was a struggle between a state with "respon-

---

3 See above, p. 133.
4 Art. 76 describes the basic objectives of the trusteeship system as:
    a. to further international peace and security;
    b. to promote the political, economic, social and educational advancement of the inhabitants of the trust territories, and their progressive development towards self-government or independence as may be appropriate to the particular circumstances of each territory and its peoples and the freely expressed wishes of the peoples concerned, and as may be provided by the terms of each trusteeship agreement;
    c. to encourage respect for human rights and for fundamental freedoms for all without distinction as to race, sex, language, or religion . . . ;
    d. to ensure equal treatment in social, economic, and commercial matters for all Members of the United Nations and their nationals, and also equal treatment for the latter in the administration of justice.

sibilities for the administration of [a territory] whose peoples have not attained a full measure of self-government" and "the inhabitants of [the territory]." It involved Article 73, without any mandate or trusteeship agreement. In exploring its ramifications, we exposed questions latent in Article 73. In accepting "as a sacred trust the obligation[s]" enumerated in Article 73, does a member of the United Nations commit itself to legal obligations? Are the obligations enforceable by proceedings in the International Court of Justice. If not, what sort of obligations are they?[5]

How might these questions come up? Conceivably, the African states may in time recover from their revulsion against the International Court of Justice in particular and against international adjudication in general. Their attention may swing from the immediate disaster which they saw in the 1966 judgment in the South West Africa cases to the potentialities discernible in the cases, highlighted by the dissenting opinions. If so, they might seek to supplement their strenuous efforts in the General Assembly to bend Portuguese policy in Angola, by a parallel endeavor in the sphere of adjudication.

One or more African states that had accepted the compulsory jurisdiction of the International Court of Justice under Article 36, paragraph 2, of the Statute of the Court might bring a proceeding against Portugal in the Court, seeking a declaratory judgment. They might ask the Court to adjudge Portugal to be in violation of paragraphs a, b, c, d, and e of Article 73 of the Charter, and to declare Portugal under a duty to modify its policies in Angola in compliance with the

5 See above, p. 48.

several paragraphs.[6] In support of their allegations and submissions, the applicant states could introduce the volumi-
nous data gathered by committees of the General Assembly.
They might also ask the Court to "entrust" the Trusteeship
Council "with the task of carrying out [any necessary or
appropriate] enquiry" and "giving an expert opinion"
pursuant to Article 50 of the Statute of the Court.

Portugal might seek to avoid the proceeding. On December 19, 1955, in the same month in which it entered the
United Nations, Portugal accepted the compulsory jurisdiction of the International Court of Justice, subject to
stated conditions. As one condition, the Portuguese government reserved the right "to exclude from the scope of the
present declaration, at any time during its validity, any
given category or categories of disputes, by notifying the
Secretary General . . . with effect from the moment of such
notification." Portugal might attempt to invoke the foregoing condition to exclude the proceeding from the scope of
its acceptance of the jurisdiction of the Court. It would be
unsuccessful, unless it exercised its reserved right prior to
the filing of the application against it. But if it did manage
to move in time, the Court would lack jurisdiction over the
defendant, and the proceeding would fail. Such a failure
would signify only what we have taken for granted through-
out these chapters. International law is a consensual system,
and the jurisdiction of international tribunals rests upon
consent. As I remarked in the second chapter, if states should
want no part of international law or international adjudication, that would end the matter.

6 For the text of Art. 73, see above, pp. 46-47.

Suppose, however, that Portugal should choose to respond within the scope of its general acceptance of the compulsory jurisdiction of the Court. It could interpose defenses comparable to those put forward by South Africa in the South West Africa cases. Portugal could object that the applicants lacked standing, on the asserted ground that they had alleged no impairment of any legal right or interest of their own, but were presuming to proceed in a representative capacity in behalf of the United Nations and the international community. Portugal could also object that insofar as paragraphs a to d, inclusive, of Article 73 prescribed standards to govern its conduct as a state administering a non-self-governing territory, they did so in terms too broad for judicial cognizance. We may assume that Portugal would carry its objections even further, protesting that Article 73 neither embodied nor was intended to embody an obligation in a contractual sense. In subscribing to Article 73 as a part of the Charter, Portugal would insist that it had merely avowed a purpose and proclaimed a policy.

The objections would be more persuasive and harder to resist than their counterparts filed by South Africa, even for judges in harmony with the outlook of the dissenters in the South West Africa cases. On the point of standing, the applicants could summon to their support the doctrine affirmed by Judge Jessup that international law "has long recognized that States may have legal interests in matters which do not affect their financial, economic, or other 'material' . . . interests" and that states may assert "a legal interest in the general observance of the rules of international law" as well as "the observance in the territories of another State, of general welfare treaty provisions."[7] But they could cite no specific source of standing comparable to the stipulation in Article 7 of the mandate that "any dispute whatever . . . between the Mandatory and another Member of the League . . . relating to the interpretation or the application of the provisions of the Mandate . . . shall be submitted to the [Court]." In regard to the other objections, the language of paragraphs a to d of Article 73 does appear to be broader and more general than the terms of the second paragraph of Article 2 of the mandate over South West Africa. The context also is more general, for it comprehends all states that are members of the United Nations and all non-self-governing territories to which the Charter might apply. The consequences of so large a frame of reference may be illuminated by an illustrative contrast.

Suppose that Portugal were to enter into a trusteeship agreement affecting Angola, in which as trustee it assumed the several obligations set forth in Article 76 of the Charter[8] in the very language of the article, together with a duty to transmit regular reports. While the scope of the undertakings in such a trusteeship agreement would be substantially identical with the scope of paragraphs a to e of Article 73, the context would be narrower and more sharply defined. It would be focused on a single specified country, Portugal, and a single specified non-self-governing territory, Angola. When used in so restricted a context, the same words would have a more limited range of possible variations in meaning,

7 South West Africa Cases, Preliminary Objections, ICJ Rep. 1962, pp. 319, 425, 428 (Dec. 21, 1962).

8 For the text of Article 76, see note 4 on p. 149.

and the burden of interpretation would be correspondingly reduced. Within the limits of such a trusteeship agreement, a court that shared the judicial philosophy of the dissenting judges in the 1966 South West Africa judgment might assert jurisdiction over the subject matter and exercise its jurisdiction.

At least, it might do so up to a point. The undertaking to transmit regular reports to the Secretary General would be sufficiently specific to pose no problem for judicial enforcement. It would be the other undertakings, more sweeping and varied in their scope than the second paragraph of Article 2 of the mandate over South West Africa, that would create difficulties. The Court would recognize that their terms would vest broad discretion in Portugal, as the trustee. Yet it might be prepared to take jurisdiction to review Portugal's exercise of discretion, if not to an extent comparable to that contemplated in Judge Jessup's dissenting opinion in the 1966 South West Africa judgment, then at least for possible abuses of discretion or bad faith.

Absent such a trusteeship agreement, I gravely doubt that even such a court would take jurisdiction over the subject matter in a proceeding brought by African states against Portugal under paragraphs a to d of Article 73 itself. I should expect the Court to allow one or both of the hypothetical objections which I have assumed Portugal would file in addition to its objection to the applicants' standing. The Court might find the terms of paragraphs a, b, c, and d too vague for judicial enforcement. It might decide that these paragraphs sound in political terms rather than legal, incorporating declarations of intention rather than contractual commitments. In either event, insofar as the dispute turned on paragraphs a to d of Article 73, it would lie beyond the reach of international adjudication. It would fall within the sphere of political action.

Yet political action need not be of a kind that has marked the deliberations of the General Assembly and the Security Council more than once during the past few years. There could be political action infused with what I have called a sense of law.

III

We come to a sort of postscript: It carries us beyond the plan of this book, which contemplated an exploration of how far international adjudication may be relevant to the settlement of the two primary types of dispute that plague contemporary international life. In moving beyond adjudication to political decisions made with a sense of law, we will keep our present focus upon conflicts between modern industrial states and newly emerging states or peoples who "have not yet attained a full measure of self-government."

In explaining what I mean by political decisions made in the spirit of law, it may be well to begin with an illustration in reverse, citing an example of international diplomacy untouched by any sense of law. It represents the manipulative meaning of "political" action, governed exclusively by estimates of immediate unilateral national or personal advantage. The example is taken from the Emergency Session of the General Assembly in June 1967, on the war in the Middle East; I quote from a commentary by James B. Reston in the *New York Times* of June 23, 1967:

> . . . the Russian argument that Israel mobilized on the Syrians' frontier in mid-May is the biggest fish story since Jonah and the whale. The Israeli Government invited the Russians to check the facts for themselves, but they preferred the lie and refused to investigate.
>
> The Arab invention that the American, rather than the Israeli, air force won the war was at least an audacious fake, worthy of that authentic phony, Herr Dr. Goebbels, but it was such obvious trash that not even the Russians believed it.
>
> Even President de Gaulle . . . seems to be losing his touch. "The [Middle East] war was started in Vietnam through American intervention," he says in his latest pronunciamento . . .
>
> Even the most obvious five-flushers here have lost their zip. They used to rush up to the podium at the General Assembly and roar out their forgeries as if they actually believed them, but now they neither pretend nor expect conviction.
>
> Maybe this is progress. At least the contemporary misrepresentations, while shameless, are more candid, but something else has happened that is not so good. A subtle change has come over the delegates in this emergency meeting of the Assembly. They may not be as gullible as their predecessors, but they are far more tolerant of falsehood and deceit than they were a few years ago. The big change is their present cynicism and moral indifference.

If Mr. Reston's description may seem caustic on its face, it will appear accurate and not intemperate to the many who heard the Emergency Session debates on television and radio broadcasts.

The fears and passions that engender such a performance are all too familiar. In the aftermath of the holocaust of World War I, Georges Clemenceau observed: "The glory of our civilization is that it enables us—occasionally—to live an almost normal life."[9] But it is not provided in the essence of things that governments must take a narrow or short-run view of national needs and purposes. National interests are no less national when they coincide with the interests of other states. It is the recognition of common needs and purposes that makes constructive diplomacy possible. The Charter of the United Nations has possibly no aspect more significant than its embodiment of agreed interests and purposes, expressly formulated.

If we take it that Article 73 of the Charter speaks in political terms, incorporating declarations of policy and statements of intention rather than contractual obligations, the declarations and statements remain expressions of policy and intention to which the member states have freely subscribed. The statements and declarations are reciprocal. They were made with the understanding that member states would take them into account in charting the respective national courses. They involve a certain kind and measure of mutual commitment and reliance, reflecting practical mutual expectations, even if neither contractual nor in the nature of estoppel.

[9] Georges Clemenceau, *Grandeur and Misery of Victory*, trans. F. M. Atkinson (New York: Harcourt, Brace and Company, 1930), p. 105.

It would not import an indifference to national interests to give due weight to those national interests that are shared with others. In deliberating on choices of national policy affecting relations between modern industrial states and newly emerging states or non-self-governing peoples, the criteria of realism and responsibility do not oblige statesmen to confine themselves to estimates of possible short-run unilateral national advantage. It would serve the requirements of responsibility and realism at least as well, especially in the long term, to try also to vindicate the common needs and purposes articulated in the Charter and the reciprocal expectations represented by Article 73. In the degree to which statesmen may do so, they will make political decisions infused with a sense of law.

I have implied a distinction that is more than verbal between a sense of law and a sense of honor and morality. Some may question the reality or significance of the distinction. The concepts overlap, of course, and in many circumstances they may be used interchangeably. But I believe the distinction is real though subtle and that it will serve a useful purpose to insist on it. To do so may sharpen our awareness of the outlook and attitudes that nourish the roots of judicial behavior and perhaps enable us in some small measure to instill some of the attitude into the political process.

In another context and indirectly, the late Dag Hammarskjøld illuminated the subject for us. He had been battered by the "troika" proposal of the Soviet Union for a divided Secretariat, in which one Secretary General would be named to represent the West, another to represent the Communist states, and a third to represent the "nonaligned states."

Khrushchev sought to justify the Soviet Union's proposal with his picturesque observation that "while there are neutral coutries, there are no neutral men." In a lecture at Oxford University on May 30, 1961, Hammarskjøld undertook to explain the international civil servant to Khrushchev and others of like mind. Hammarskjøld poured his heart and mind into the effort:

> . . . it may be said that he [the international civil servant] will carefully seek guidance in the decisions of the main organs, in statements relevant for the interpretation of those decisions, in the Charter and in generally recognized principles of law, remembering that by his actions he may set important precedents . . . Even if all of these steps are taken, it will still remain . . . that the reduced area of discretion will be large enough to expose the international Secretariat to heated political controversy and to accusations of a lack of neutrality.
>
> I have already drawn attention to the ambiguity of the word "neutrality" in such a context. It is obvious from what I have said that the international civil servant cannot be accused of lack of neutrality simply for taking a stand on a controversial issue when this is his duty and cannot be avoided. But there remains a serious intellectual and moral problem as we move within an area inside which personal judgment must come into play. Finally, we have to deal here with a question of integrity or with, if you please, a question of conscience.
>
> The international civil servant must keep himself

under the strictest observation. He is not requested to be a neuter in the sense that he has to have no sympathies or antipathies, that there are to be no interests which are close to him in his personal capacity, or that he is to have no ideas or ideals that matter for him. However, he is requested to be fully aware of those human reactions and meticulously check himself so that they are not permitted to influence his actions. This is nothing unique. Is not every judge professionally under the same obligation?[10]

I do not intimate that a national politician or diplomat either can or should act like an international civil servant or a judge. I do consider that the characteristics of an international civil servant delineated by Hammarskjøld reflect the former's total and exclusive commitment to the common objectives of the member states incorporated in the principles and purposes of the Charter. I also think that Hammarskjøld's perception of some points of psychological affinity between the international civil servant and the judge are acute and profound. In confronting disputes within the ambit of Chapters XI and XII of the Charter, a national politician or diplomat may well adopt elements of the international civil servant's and judge's attitude as a part of his own, and blend it with the other appropriate aspects of his own characteristic pattern of behavior. I believe it would be

10 Dag Hammarskjøld, *The International Civil Servant in Law and Fact* (Lecture delivered to the Congregation on May 30, 1961; Oxford: Clarendon Press, 1961), pp. 26-27. Reprinted in Wilder Foote, ed., *Dag Hammarskjøld, Servant of Peace* (New York and Evanston: Harper & Row, 1962), pp. 329, 347-348.

wise and constructive, as well as realistic and responsive to his duty, for him to do so.

If such political behavior should become customary in the General Assembly or the Security Council, we may safely predict that the James B. Restons of the future will sing another tune. I am confident they would be happy to do so.

INDEX

Adjudication, *see* Justiciability
Air Transport Services Agreement (USA-France), 50-51, 55
Apartheid (in South West Africa Cases, Second Phase), 129-136, 141
Arab states, *see* United Nations, General Assembly and Middle East
Asylum case, 119

Badawi, Judge, 102
Buchanan, Pres. James, 14-16, 17, 18
Bustamante, Judge, 102

Charitable trusts, 89-91
Churchill, Winston, 40
Civil War (USA), issues in legal aspect, 11-20
Clémenceau, Georges, 157
Cold War dispute, meaning, nature, patterns of behavior, 7-11, 36, 37, 39-40, 41
Contracts, varieties, compared with treaties, 55-56

Ethiopia, 82, 84, 85, 87, 88, 89, 93, 146, 148. *See also* South West Africa Cases

Fitzmaurice, Judge Gerald, 93-96, 97, 103, 130
Forster, Judge, 128, 131, 135

General Assembly, *see* United Nations
General Assembly Resolutions: No. 1514, 58-59, 60, 115, 122, 123; No. 1541, 59; No. 1542, 59; No. 1654, 59; No. 1810, 60, 115; No. 2145,

105-106, 110, 111, 115, 116, 123, 124, 125, 127, 140; No. 2248, 106-110, 124, 125, 127
Gordon, Hawaii v., 29n
Gross, Leo, 66-67

Hammarskjøld, Dag, 159-160
Hawaii v. Gordon, 29n
Herter, Christian A., 2

Inter-American Treaty of Reciprocal Assistance, 8-9
International civil servant, 159-160. *See also* Secretariat
International Court of Justice: Statute, 36, 38-39, 77, 92, 102, 111, 119, 128, 136, 138, 141, 150, 151; advisory opinions, 64-67, 76-78, 79-80, 85, 105, 111, 112, 140-141; rules, 84, 128; succeeds P.C.I.J. under Mandate over South West Africa, 86, 111, 112, 113, 138, 141, 148; UN as party in, 92; relation to UN, 97-99; changes in membership, 102; enforcement of judgment, 139, 141, 142. *See also* South West Africa, South West Africa Cases
International law: evolution, 3-6; twentieth-century adjustments, 3-4; setting of Cold War disputes, 8-10, 41; relation to disputes between colonial peoples and colonial powers, 41. *See also* International Court of Justice; International organizations; South West Africa Cases; United Nations
International organizations: evolu-